PERFORMANCE OF WOMEN POLICE

PERFORMANCE OF WOMEN POLICE

TAMIL NADU

A.P. MOHAMED ALI

Publications

KALPAZ PUBLICATIONS
Delhi - 110052

Performance of Women Police : Tamil Nadu

ISBN : 81-7835-574-4

Rs. 690

Published in 2006 in India by
Kalpaz Publications
C-30, Satyawati Nagar,
Delhi - 110052
e-mail : kalpaz@hotmail.com

Laser Typesetting at : Vinayak Printers, Delhi
Printed at : Salasar Imaging System, Delhi

Dedication

My parents have nurtured, groomed and educated me that I have grown up to be what I am today. My sense of gratitude knows no bounds when I realize that the fruits of such excellent upbringing have evolved into many remarkable milestones in my life and career. I therefore, humbly dedicate my research work to my loving (late) parents.

I owe a great deal to my beloved wife who has been treading patiently by my side and has been extending immense moral support. I also dedicate this work to my loving wife.

A.P. Mohamed Ali

Contents

Foreward

Punditry in Police is a rare commodity. Time was when bulk of the Police Force could hardly read and write. But things have changed and in Tamil Nadu. We have more members in all ranks holding Post Graduate Degrees and Doctorates than in any other Police Force. Mohamed Ali has displayed not only true academic virtues but rare imagination in exploring a hitherto virgin area of performance of women police and evaluating their contribution, of course, limiting his study to Tamil Nadu. It is a fascinating subject and that apart, it is necessary to evaluate the employment of women in Police Force in large numbers so that what began as an experiment can be an important part of the system. Mohamed Ali's work is timely because it is a little over 25 years when Tamil Nadu started recruiting women into Police Force in sizeable numbers. I would like to record here my warmest admiration and tribute to the great former Chief Minister, Dr. M.G. Ramachandran who took a giant step in ordering enlistment of women police in hundreds when more timid and conservative men like me were a little scared. It was entirely a new scenario and the study by Mohamed Ali reveals that some of our fears were not unfounded but solutions were also easily available. The result - a people friendly police.

The findings also highlight the, not wholly satisfactory working conditions, poor facilities, sometimes overbearing interference from male superiors, subtle gender discriminations and above all, nagging domestic problems. On this point, I remember to have had some long discussions with the senior officers of British Police and they had the same story to tell. But the benefits of opening the doors to women are immense and they have given a totally new philosophy for the police. One cannot, but agree with Mohamed Ali when he points his fingers at numerous deficiencies in working facilities for women in the Police Force which need urgent attention. Pick-up and drop transport facilities, rest room and gym and mini kitchen, basic health kit are all available in modern police station in the developed world but tragically absent in India. This thesis which has resulted in the award of "DEGREE OF DOCTOR OF PHILOSOPHY" is worth its weight in gold. It should be read by the powers that be including the legislators, and that exercise should reflect in the next police budget. Then the girls in uniform will be happy members of the police and its jewels.

I'm grateful to Dr. A.P. Mohamed Ali for giving me this rare honour of writing a Foreward. I have not done full justice for I was hard-pressed for time and my secretary was whispering all the time I might miss the flight. Lufthansa is no respector of persons.

V.R. Lakshminarayanan, I.P.S.
Director General of Police (Retd.)

Preface

Maintenance of Law and Order, ensuring peace and tranquility in the society and protection of the lives and properties are the main functions of the democracy. The primary task of the police is preserving the internal security of any country. In addition, the Police have to deal with the social evils involving women and also to overcome the problems arose out of women criminals. The Legislators and Administrators found out that the women are possessed with the natural qualities of comforting the destitutes, combating women criminals and counseling the domestic problems. Further the right to work and clamour for equal rights and responsibilities from women forced the Administrators to employ women police in the Police Department.

Even though our ancient scriptures like Ramayana, Mahabharata, Arthasastra and Emperor Asoka edicts speak about the employing of women in the harem spies, the actual employment of women police in India was thought of while dealing with women agitators in Kanpur Labour strike in 1938. Now the women police have become part and parcel of Labour Force in almost every state. The enrolling of woman in Tamil Nadu had started in 1973 and it had achieved in having as the largest state in India. Since its inception no attempts were made to evaluate the performance of women police from the consumer point of view, that's the bird's view of the citizen, who interact with the women police. My natural urge with the god educational background took up the task of undertaking the research under the able and efficient guidance of then Vice-Chancellor of Tiruvelveli Manonmaniam Sundaranar University and now the Professor of crime and victimology in Tokiwa International University, Japan, Dr. K. Chockalingam. The University of Madras awarded Doctorate of Philosophy on 30-11-04.

My family and friends suggested to publish the thesis as a book. My request to Gyan Books Pvt. Ltd., New Delhi, was received with positive and Tr. AMIT GARG, the Director, publications, to extend heartfelt cooperation to encourage me in publication. My special thanks to Kalpaz Publications for finalizing the agreement. Above all I express gratitude to Mr. V.R. Lakshminarayanan, D.G.P. (Retd.), human rights activist and younger brother of Great Jurist Mr. V.R. Krishna Iyyer, for penning the 'Forward Note'.

I hope that the book on hand my enlighten the public the working environment of women police, problems faced by them in surmounting the crisis within the family, department and society, shortcomings in service, consumer level of satisfaction and also their expectations. Any suggestion and constructive criticism from the readers will be graciously received.

Acknowledgements

First of all I must thank my one time Madras University P.G. Hostel mate and learned Professor of Criminology and Erudite Scholar of Victimology and presently Vice Chancellor of Manonmaniam Sundaranar University, Tirunelveli *Dr. K. Chockalingam,* for having given me an opportunity to work for my doctoral research under his guidance, that too, in the subject related to the Police Department. When I suggested the present study of evaluation of the performance of Women Police in Tamil Nadu, he encouraged and guided me with his rich experience and high academic excellence. Several valuable hours of his time, in the midst of his national and international obligations, he spared for me in discussions and in going through the many drafts of the manuscript of the thesis are proof for his insistence on quality work, which I acknowledge with gratitude.

I express my gratitude to *Dr. M. Srinivasan,* Lecturer, Department of Criminology, University of Madras for his continued support which helped me in the successful completion of my research work.

I am thankful to *Dr. T. Anbupazham,* Lecturer in Statistics, University of Madras and *Prof. M. Saravanan, M.S.,* Computer Analyst, IIT, Chennai for helping me in the statistical analysis of data.

I express my sincere thanks to the assistance

rendered by *Selvi R. Bindu, Selvi G. Jayanthi, Ms. S. Grace Nesamoney* and enthusiastic students of Criminology department, University of Madras for their continued co-operation in collecting the data.

A word of special thanks is forwarded to *Mr. C.V. Vishnu Prasad,* Police Personnel. I thank various authors whose writings have been utilised for the references and guidances who computerised the data and also typed the entire work.

A.P. Mohamed Ali

1

Introduction

Preservation of peace and protection of life and property are the basic needs in a democratic society. Since each citizen cannot assume individual responsibility for the fulfillment of these needs, various Governments have employed the police forces to preserve and protect the rights and properties of citizens. In carrying out these duties, the police officers come to realise the problems of citizens whose welfare and safety are jeopardized by the lawless, the greedy and the irresponsible. The police mostly have to deal with complex and serious problems of murder, robbery and assault. In addition, the police have to deal with problems connected to cases of neglect, destitution, abandonment and other personal difficulties also. In dealing with these problems, the police come across many children and women, involved in crimes both as victims and as offenders. During the course, the police officials have learnt that patient hearing and sympathetic understanding are needed to solve these problems. As the women police possess these qualities in abundance, they were found to be more successful than their male counterparts in investigation of crimes concerning women and children (Krishnamurthi, 1996).

The need for women police was first recognized in the United States, during the firsthalf of the nineteenth century, when "Police Matrons" were appointed in New York City in 1845, for handling of women and girls held in police custody, by the law enforcing agency. The earliest appointment of a police woman, as distinguished from a police matron, was made in Chicago, in 1893. In 1903, women police were officially employed for the first time in Stuttgart (Federal Republic of Germany) and in 1905, a woman was given police powers in Portland, Oregon (USA), to deal effectively with problems involving girls and children. In 1910, the first regularly rated police women were appointed by the Los Angeles Police Department. The First World War provided an opportunity for women to serve as volunteer workers and part-time workers to demonstrate, in a conspicuous manner, their usefulness in police work. The Metropolitan Women Police was formed in London in 1919 (Rao et al., 1975).

In India, early history of policing by women is available in the Ramayana, Mahabharata, 'Arthashastra' of Kautilya and the Ashokan edicts. The Ramayana gives a vivid description of how Sita was put under surveillance of the police women who carried all round vigil. Likewise, the Ashokan edicts frequently speak about the 'Prativedikas' who protected the Royal chambers from intruders and kept the king informed about the day to day happenings and often escorted important cellers [Roy, 1999].

Kautilya, the most perfect Raj Guru, in his magnum opus the "Arthashastra" stated that the king must employ women for policing and spying in the garb of "Vishkanyas" or poison girls. Spies from the categories of "Bhikshukies" were recruited to report the rebel and enemy activities to the king. Hence, policing i.e., helping to maintain law and order by women is not an alien concept for us [*Saxena, 1983*]. More than Manu's social code, it was the spell of Mughal Feudal Aristocracy, which had driven the Indian women behind the veil and condemned them to the drudgery of men, children and household chores. However, due to the socio-economic reforms initiated by visionaries like Raja Ram Mohan Roy, Swami Dayanand Saraswati and Mahatma Gandhi, the situation has changed radically today. The worldwide liberation of women compelled the Indian Society to yield the places of responsibility to women in various areas of life that were previously considered as male bastions. Today, women are performing with dynamism, credibility and spirit in all areas of public life.

In India, the need for women police was first felt during the labour strike, which took place in Kanpur, in the year 1938. The State of Travancore also experimented with the appointment of women as Special Police Constables, in the year 1933. One woman head constable and twelve women police constables were then appointed as Special Police Constables (Rao et al., 1975). Excepting these places, policewomen were unknown in India (Govt. of India, 1981). The partition of India in 1947, in its wake brought endless misery, squalor and moral degradation. The honour and security of women became a problem. Kidnapping, abduction and sex offences showed a marked increase. Relief camps had been started for unattached women, girls and children whose male members had been mercilessly killed. Young girls who were kidnapped, raped, forcibly converted or sold at the auction block were recovered. As a result, women organisations cropped up. The Ministry of Relief and Rehabilitation also needed women police for the recovery of abducted women and girls. From all the above instances, it is evident that the need for women police was felt strongly. With the passage of time, when a number of social legislations were enacted for women and children, new avenues opened up where women police were better suited. The rate of increase in the criminality by women and juvenile criminality also necessitated the use of women police (*Ghosh, 1981*).

Women Police in Modern Society

Modern society has evolved from the conflicts between the traditional and modern, the rational and irrational. Old relationships and taboos are being broken and new patterns are emerging. The category of people suffering the most, because of this traumatic transformation, women all over the world have had to struggle hard, to make a breakthrough into the police service. It is the same story in every country. It took years before they could overcome male resistance - the main hurdle in their way. Men were neither prepared to induct women straightaway into the police force nor did they like to share power with them. At first they entrusted women with a very limited role in cases relating to women and children. Most of the departments tried the tentative employment of a few women, often untrained and without police powers for selected duties. Close on the heels came recognition of their value in dealing with important cases relating to women and children. After realizing the advantages of the system, they were given police training and police powers (Barbara, 1985).

By the 1970's, women had broken the legal and practical barriers to enter into police departments. Despite skepticism and hostility, they demonstrated that they were as capable as men in handling routine police tasks. Several research studies revealed no consistent differences in the quality of men's and women's performance on the street (Bloch and Anderson, 1974; Price, 1974; Sherman, 1975; Townsey, 1982). Many police officers and supervisors, as well as casual observers and scholars, nonetheless, believe that men and women bring to the job, differences in attitudes, values and perceptions that influence, albeit in subtle ways, the way in which they do their work. When women were first accepted into the police departments at the turn of the century, their roles were restricted to what were thought to be as the feminine tasks of dealing with juveniles, families and female offenders and providing clerical support to male officers (Price and Gavin, 1982). The Police administrators, patrol officers and the public believed that women were unsuited both physically and temperamentally for the rigors of "real" police work (Flynn, 1982 and Martin, 1980).

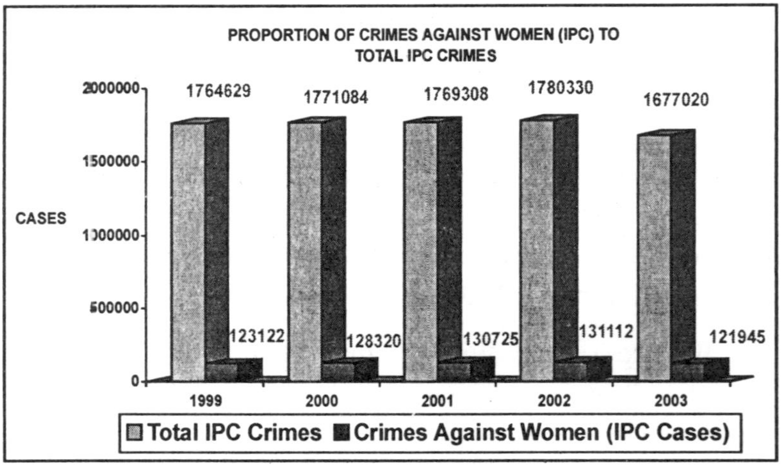

Fig. 1. Proportion of Crimes Against Women (Indian Penal Code Crimes) to Total Indian Penal Code Crimes.

In a situation where policing is by men, women are discriminated against and suffer ignominies, men become the helpless spectators when women go on a law-breaking spree. As a result, in the last three decades crimes against women and by them have increased alarmingly.

In a country like India, the problem of policing has taken an entirely new dimension due to the rapidly changing socio-economic and political conditions. In several states, increasing involvement

Table 1. Number of Crimes Against Women to Total IPC Crimes

Sr. No.	*Year*	*Total IPC Crimes*	*Crimes Against women (IPCcases)*	*Percentage to total IPC Crimes*
1.	1999	17,64629	1,23,122	7.0
2.	2000	17,71084	1,28,320	7.2
3.	2001	17,69,308	1,30,72 5	7.4
4.	2002	17,80,330	1,31,112	7.4
5.	2003	16,77,020	1,21,945	7.3

Source: Crime in India, 2003.

and participation of women in various political agitations, riots, student demonstrations have become a regular feature. This aspect has put extra strain on the police force, particularly keeping in mind the problem of handling women, while enforcing law.

The increasing involvement of women in crime, delinquency, deviancy and agitations stresses the need for developing women police units, suitably trained in the tasks attuned to them (Rao et al., 1975) and also to deal with sensitive problems relating to juvenile delinquency and maladjustment.

Though the status of women in policing, of late, has been considered indispensable, the use of their potentialities are yet inadequate, sidelined and stagnant. It is a hundred years since women entered the police field but even today, they are not considered as equals to their male counterparts. As such, till date, in many vital areas of police work, women police remain underutilized and under estimated (Krishnamurthi, 1996).

Table 2. Year of Entry of Women Police in the States/Union Territories in India.

Sl. No.	*Name of States/ Union Territories*	*Year of Initial appointment*
1.	Andhra Pradesh	1950 (Erstwhile State of Hyderabad)
2.	Arunachal Pradesh	1977
3.	Assam	1969
4.	Bihar	1952
5.	Chandigarh	1977
6.	Delhi	1948
7.	Gujarat	1948/49 Authentic information not available)
8.	Himachal Pradesh	1975
9.	Jammu & Kashmir	1965
10.	Karnataka	1960
11.	Kerala	1943
12.	Madhya Pradesh	1953
13.	Maharashtra	1939 (Greater Bombay)
14.	Manipur	1961
15.	Meghalaya	1976
16.	Mizoram	1987
17.	Nagaland	1968
18.	Orissa	1961
19.	Pondicherry	1974
20.	Punjab	1948 (Correct information Not available)
21.	Rajasthan	1955
22.	Sikkim	1970
23.	Tamil Nadu	1973
24.	Tripura	1961
25.	Uttar Pradesh	1974/67 (Correct information Not available)

Sources: (i) Information available from the State Government (only 11 states)
(ii) Bureau of Police Research and Development, New Delhi.

Functions and Role of Women Police in India

In India, the history of women police is not different from that of women police in other countries. In India, as in many other countries, women entered the police service primarily to deal with other women. The need to have women police, increased with the rising number of women accused, criminals and victims of crime (Mahajan, 1982).

At the XXVIth Session of the General Assembly of International Criminal Police Commission held in Lisbon, Portugal from 17-22, June 1957, the duties of the women police were classified as:

(i) Preventive Duties

Like discovering neglected, abandoned wayward children and juveniles without occupation or with a tendency to become prostitutes; teaching and helping school children to deal with traffic rules and regulations.

(ii) Administrative Duties

Searching runaway and absconding children; establishing card index system for minors and females; and as liasion in providing social, medical and school services.

(iii) Supportive Duties

Investigations of juvenile delinquents of both sexes and young women offenders; interrogation of children, adolescents and sensitive women; detection of clandestine prostitutes and searching arrested women (Ghosh, 1981).

According to a Bureau of Police Research and Development report (1975), some of the principal duties to be performed by women police in India are:

- Helping in the investigation of crimes involving women and children.
- Providing assistance to the local police in tracing missing women and children.
- Recovering minor girls from brothels and escorting them to rescue homes, courts and hospitals.
- Recovery of women and girls involved in abduction and kidnapping cases; collection of intelligence, interrogation of juveniles, women offenders, under trials and witnesses.
- Search and escort of women offenders.
- VIP and security duties.
- Work relating to women passengers at airports and search of their person and belongings.
- Providing assistance to the local police in evacuating women and children from disturbed areas during emergencies.
- Further, women police can perform duties in maintaining order in women's meetings and processions.
- Dealing with women agitators, satyagrahis and labour troubles in which women are involved.
- Looking after women and children at fairs and in places of pilgrimage during festivals.

- Guiding women passengers at big railway stations and important bus stands in large towns and cities and
- Helping children to cross roads near schools.

An empirical study conducted by Aleem (1991) revealed that women police have been found very useful in the investigation of cases pertaining to rape, unnatural deaths of women; family disputes; juvenile delinquency and immoral trafficking in women. She has further indicated that though there is a long list of functions, including traffic duties, which can be entrusted to the women police, in reality, they are given very few functions. Generally, women police are not given independent charge of investigating crimes of sexual abuse, rape and dowry deaths. In most of the crimes committed by or against women, women police are used only as assistants to their male counterparts, wherever needed but not as an independent identity.

Even today in all the States, women police (except those in the higher police service such as Indian Police Service) are basically entrusted with functions pertaining to women. States like Andhra Pradesh, Madhya Pradesh and Delhi have experimented with extending the scope of their functions by entrusting them with the responsibilities of a Station House Officer. Nevertheless these are exceptions. While some States have prepared a long list of duties, others have described only a few of them.

The Delhi police have listed the duties of women police as follows:

- Attending to complaints as duty officers in the reporting rooms of police stations
- Escorting female accused/under trials to the court/lock-up
- Interrogating women victims in cases of rape, unnatural death of women, family disputes and
- Performing law and order duties

In Arunachal Pradesh, the functions assigned to women police are:

- Frisking women passengers at airports.
- Searching/arresting of women accused/ suspects.
- Controlling traffic.
- Working as duty officers at police stations, and
- Interrogating women suspects.

The main functions assigned to women police in Sikkim are:

- Making General Diary entries
- Receiving and despatching files and letters
- Controlling traffic
- Performing law and order duties, and
- Assisting in cases involving women

The Governments of Andhra Pradesh, Himachal Pradesh and Karnataka have long lists of functions, as noted below, yet most of them are not performed by police women.

The following functions are assigned to women police in Andhra Pradesh:

- Helping in the investigation of offences involving women and children.
- Assisting the local police in tracing missing women and children, keeping a watch over places of ill-repute, recovering minor girls from brothels and escorting them to rescue homes, courts and hospitals and recovering women and girls involved in abduction and kidnapping cases.
- Collecting intelligence.
- Interrogating juveniles, women offenders, under trials, witnesses and juvenile victims of sexual offences.
- Arresting, searching and escorting women offenders.
- Performing VIP and other security duties.
- Performing work relating to women passengers at airports such as searching their personal belongings.
- Conducting enquiries, in connection with passport applications and family matters.
- Assisting local police in evacuating women and children from disturbed areas during emergencies, and

- Maintaining order at women's meetings and processions.

The main functions assigned to women police in the State of Himachal Pradesh are:

- Providing assistance to the male investigating officers during investigation of cases involving female suspects, witnesses and minors.
- Handling and controlling female demonstrators, female criminals indulging in unlawful acts and escorting them while in custody.
- Carrying out searches, interrogations and enquiries of women complainants/accused at the police stations.
- Dealing with cases involving juvenile offenders and helping in tracing missing women and children.
- Discharging duties at places like the police reporting rooms and checking cases of eve-teasing and harassment of women tourists.
- To be deployed at fairs and festivals to carry out duties that may be assigned to them by the authorities, keeping in view the requirements of such places.
- To be detailed with women VIPs and at other functions when required.
- To be deployed at ceremonial parades in the form of a complete reserve/platoon at important National and State celebrations like

Independence Day, Republic Day, Statehood Day and Himachal Day.

- To be deployed for duties for removal of immoral trafficking in women and to deal with women taking part in processions, demonstrations and dharnas.
- To be deployed in helping and advising women seeking police help.
- Conveying/escorting women and children to and from police stations to courts/prisons and attending to women/children in courts.
- To be employed in plain clothes for detection work and at airports for security and frisking purpose, whenever required and
- Looking after the welfare work of the families of the policemen.

The Government of Karnataka has formulated instructions [Standing Order No. 659, 9-6-75 – office of the Director General of Police and Inspector General of Police, Karnataka, Letter No. 113/QST/4187-88, dated 12.7.1988] regarding the functions to be assigned to women police.

These are:

- Collecting information regarding women offenders.
- Guarding and escorting women prisoners while in police custody.
- Arresting and searching women offenders.

- Questioning and interrogating women offenders and witnesses.
- Maintaining order at places where women congregate in large numbers, e.g., at temples, fairs, exhibitions and functions arranged by women's associations.
- Guiding women passengers at big railway stations and important bus stands in large cities and towns.
- Rescuing girls who are used for prostitution or other criminal purposes coming within the ambit of the law.
- Preventing juvenile crime.
- Rendering assistance to their male counterparts in enforcing the suppression of Immoral Traffic in Women and Girls Act 104 of 1956.
- Rendering assistance to the men police while dealing with labour troubles where women workers are involved.
- Operating telephones at the Police Stations and units during emergencies.
- Doing social work among the families of policemen in the lines, and
- Performing such other duties as may need employment of women police.

Hence, in most of the States, the women police officers perform, more or less, the following duties:

- Helping in the investigation of offences involving women and juveniles.
- Assisting the police, in tracing missing women and children, keeping a watch over the places of ill-repute, recovering minor girls from brothels and escorting them to rescue homes, courts, hospitals, jails and recovery of women and girls involved in abduction and kidnapping cases.
- Collection of intelligence.
- Interrogation of juvenile and women offenders, under trials and women witnesses.
- Assisting the police in the investigation of rape cases.
- Arrest, Search and Escort of Women and Juvenile offenders.
- Security check on women and their belongings at airports.
- Assisting women and children commuters at airports, big railway stations and bus termini.
- Conducting search on women on border checkposts.
- Looking after women and children at big fairs, festivals and places of pilgrimage.
- Dealing with women agitators and satyagrahis during political and labour demonstrations.
- Maintaining order in women's meetings and processions.
- VIP and other security duties.

- Family investigations involving women.
- Assisting social organizations and probation officers in the rehabilitation of run away women and young girls and prostitutes.
- Helping women and children to cross roads.
- Police women are given public relations work which they perform with credit.

Women police officers have the same powers as their male counterparts.

Future of Women Police in India

Police Administration like any other branch of public administration is not static but dynamic. Rao et al. (1975) has stated that a beginning must be made to throw open the doors of the police administration to researchers and experts in academic disciplines to secure a suitable and stable organization to meet the challenges of the future.

The sociological impact of women taking jobs within exclusively male territory has aroused much controversy. Traditionalists feel that, a woman's place is in the home. In recent years, however, society has accepted and women in particular have gained acceptance in areas of life hitherto zealously guarded as sacrosanct to the male (Ghosh, 1981).

Women brought a social viewpoint to police work (Higgins, 1962). The greatest contribution of the police women will be that they will raise the standard of qualification for all police officers (Baradwaj, 1976).

The best hope for the police women's future is the police woman herself (Horne, 1980). She must and should join with the policewomen in the world to speak out, to try to influence the police chief and the powers that control 'the police budget. She must be guided to realize her full potential for the benefit of law enforcement of the society.

Women Police in Tamil Nadu

In a tradition bound society of India, women are brought up in a cultural milieu which relegates them to a secondary role. The tradition, the social norms and the other unwritten codes and rules of the society make it a duty for a woman to serve the man of the house by looking after his physical and instinctual needs and she ends up subordinating herself to him by carrying out his dictates. In its dignified form, the role of a woman makes her out to be the house-wife, who looks after the comforts of her family members helping them perform their task well, but often this role deteriorates to that of a whole time servant, who can be ordered around to render service at one's beck and call.

Growing in such a socio-cultural environment and taking up at every stage of her growth, the norms, the traditions and role-expectations bound with our culture, the women of our society face a lot of psychological disadvantages while attempting to get redressal to their problems. Also, in a society where the woman carries the burden of guilt and the man goes scot free, they are afraid of making an issue of the injustice perpetrated on them for fear that facts may be distorted against them.

Due to the rapidly changing socio-economic and political conditions, a new dimension to the problem of policing in India has emerged. In several states, political and linguistic agitations, bandhs, with increasing participation of women have become a regular feature. Besides these, there is an increasing involvement of women in crime of deviance and an increase in the number of crimes committed against women. All these factors have led to an increase in the strength of the already existing women police force (Rao et al., 1975).

The Government in their order Ms. No. 2382, Home Department, dated 5th September 1975 sanctioned raising of a women police wing in the Chennai City Police with a strength of one woman Sub-Inspector, one woman Head Constable and 20 Women Police Constables.

In the same government order, they were allotted the following duties:

- Patrolling areas where undesirable women frequent.
- Rescue of young girls found homeless and in danger of becoming prostitutes.
- Accompanying the police in Immoral Traffic Act (104 of 1956) Raids.
- Escorting to court and guarding in court, female prisoners.

- Escorting remand and female under trial prisoners.
- Assisting investigating officers and questioning complainants in cases such as assaults on women and children.
- Dealing with stray children.
- Bandobust duties at large gatherings where women congregate, e.g., big public meetings and festivals where there are separate women enclosures.

Later, Government in their order Ms. No. 2566, Home Department, dated 1st November, 1974 issued adhoc rules for the following women police personnel.

- Women Sub-Inspectors
- Women Head Constables
- Women Constables

The adhoc rules deal with appointment, appointing authority, qualifications, physical measurements for direct recruitment or recruitment by transfer, training, probation, seniority, promotion, transfer and postings, applicability of discipline and Appeal Rules.

Afterwards, the Government in their order Ms. No. 1706, dated 3.7.1986 created the posts of Women Inspectors and Women Deputy Superintendents of Police.

Recruitment and Training of Women Police

The recruitment policy of an organization has a direct bearing on its efficiency, and therefore, requires careful formulation. The eligibility criteria should be so laid down that the most suitable candidates are selected. This is a very important criteria for the requirement of police personnel, who are the custodians of law and protectors of life and property of the community. Any lapse on their part can have serious repercussions on the freedom on individual citizens. The performance of the police in India has not been up to the public expectations. The police neither have a good image nor enjoy the confidence of the people. The people seem to expect a better performance from women police (Aleem, 1991).

As far as recruitment of women police in the State of Tamil Nadu is concerned, it is carried out at 3 levels. Women Police constables and Sub-Inspectors are recruited through Uniform Service Recruitment Board (USRB), an organisation responsible for recruiting personnel for all the uniformed services. Women police officers at the level of Deputy Superintendent of Police (DSP) are recruited through Tamil Nadu Police Service Commission (TNPSC). Officers at the level of Assistant Superintendent of Police (ASP) are recruited through the All India Competitive exam. Conducted by the Union Public Service Commission (UPSC), Government of India. Both Assistant Superintendent of Police and the Deputy

Superintendent of Police are called sub-division officers.

With regard to the training of Women Police the following procedures are adopted in the State of Tamil Nadu:

(a) Women police who are recruited as (Grade-II) Constables will be imparted training for a period of 6 months at police recruit schools, situated at district headquarters.

(b) Women Sub-Inspectors of Police are given training for a period of 1 year at the Police Training College, Chennai.

(c) For the officers (Deputy Superintendents of Police) a one year intensive training is given at the Police Training College, Chennai.

(d) For the Assistant Superintendents of Police who are recruited on an All Indian basis, are provided training at an All India level at the National Academy (Sardar Vallabhbhai Patel National Police Academy, Hyderabad). The total period of training is 24 months, which includes both institutional and field training.

There is no difference between male and female police officers with regard to the content, method and period of training at all levels.

The discrepancy in the strength of the police in the lower ranks with regard to the sanctioned strength versus actual strength is only a transitory phase. The vacancies have to be filled up after going

Table 3. Special Quotas

1.	Sports Quota	Existing 10% quota shall continue. If it is not possible to fill up the sports quota of 10% the gap be filled up by the dependents of the serving personnel.
2.	Quota for the dependents of serving police personnel	*10% quota under direct recruitment for dependents of the serving police personnel and the wards/dependents of retired, deceased and medically invalidated police personnel.

* Note: The total percentage of above quotas should not exceed 20%.

Table 4. Qualification: (i) Women Sub-Inspectors

Sl. No.	*Parameters*	*Qualificati on/Method/Procedure of Recruitment*	
1.	Age	20-28 Years	
	Age Relaxation	Scheduled Caste/ Scheduled Tribe	— 33 Years
		Ex-Service men	— Within three years from the date of discharge subject to a maximum of 45 years.
		Destitute Widows belonging to open competition/ Backward class/Most Backward class/Denotified communities/ Scheduled Caste/ Scheduled Tribe	35 Years
2.	Minimum Height	157 Centimeters	
	Height Relaxation	Scheduled Caste/ Scheduled Tribe	— 155 Centimeters
3.	Educational Qualifications	Any Degree	

(contd.)

Sl. No.	*Parameters*	*Qualificati on/Method/Procedure of Recruitment*
4.	Physical Efficiency Test	ENDURANCE TEST: Running 400 meters in 12C seconds. Successful candidates have to undergo Physical Efficiency Test as follows: 3 events with a minimum qualifying marks of 9 (1 star in two events and 2 stars in one event) and a maximum of 15 Marks.
5.	Written Test	Minimum Qualifying Marks: 35 Marks out of 75 Marks
6.	Viva Voce	Viva Voce - 10 Marks

Table 5. (ii) Women Police Constables

Sl. No.	*Parameters*	*Qualification/Method/Procedure of Recruitment*		
1.	Age	18-24 Years		
	Age Relaxation	Scheduled Caste/Scheduled Tribe	—	29 Years
		Ex-Service men	—	Within three years from the date of discharge subject to a maximum of 45 years.
		Destitute Widows belonging to open competition/ Backward class/Most Backwa rd class/Denotified communities/ Scheduled Caste/ Scheduled Tribe		35 Years
2.	Minimum Height	157 Centimeters		
	Height Relaxation	Scheduled Caste/ Scheduled Tribe	—	155 Centimeters
3.	Educational Qualifications	Tenth Standard or Secondary School Leaving Certificate (SSLC)(Old Pattern)		

(contd.)

Sl. No.	*Parameters*	*Qualification/Method/Procedure of Recruitment*
4.	Physical Efficiency Test	PHYSICAL ENDURANCE TEST: Running 400 meters in 120 Seconds. Successful candidates have to undergo Physical Efficiency Test As follows: 3 events with a minimum qualifying marks of 6 (Minimum 1 star in each event)
5.	Written Test	Minimum Qualifying Marks: 40 Marks out of 85 Marks
6.	Viva Voce	Viva Voce dispensed with

Source: "Handbook on Police, Tamil Nadu - 2003", Statistical Section, Office of the Director General of Police, Chennai-4.

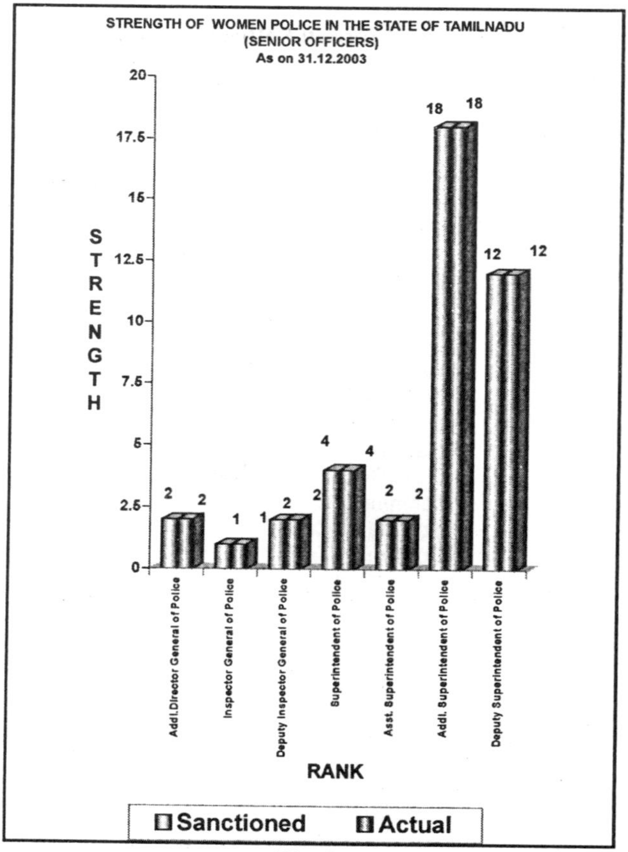

Fig. 2.

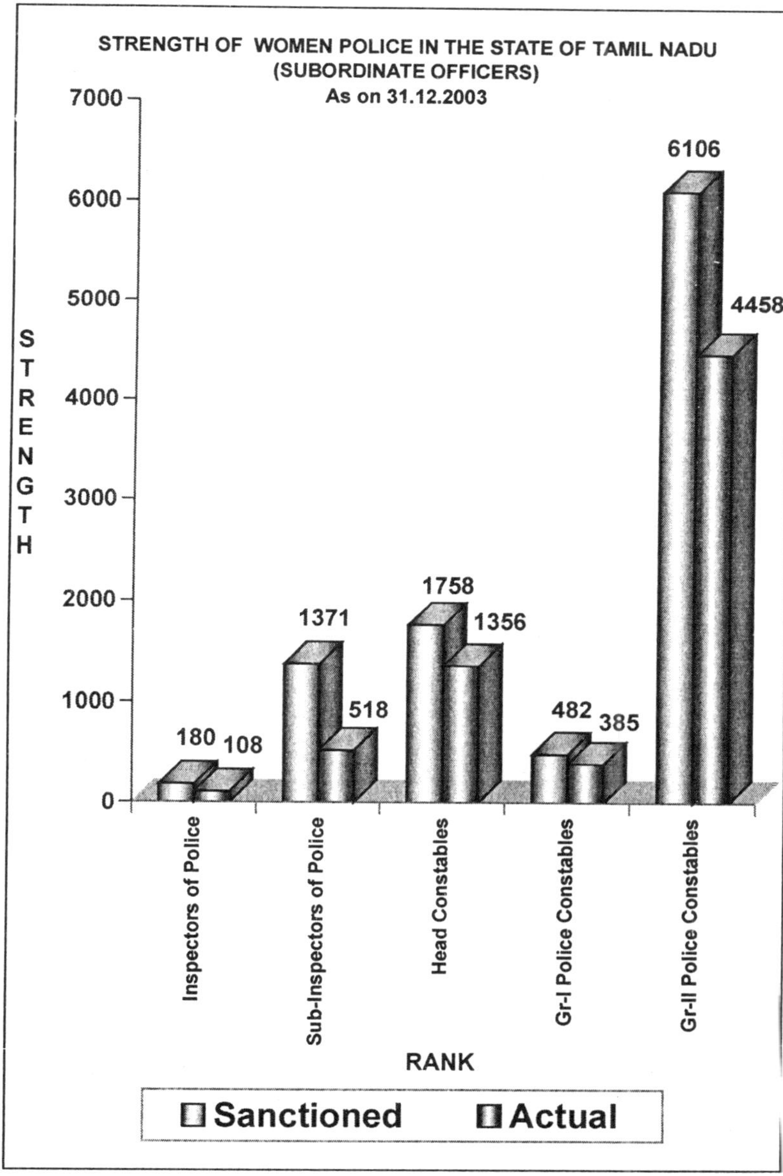
STRENGTH OF WOMEN POLICE IN THE STATE OF TAMIL NADU
(SUBORDINATE OFFICERS)
As on 31.12.2003
STRENGTH
7000
6000
5000
4000
3000
2000
1000
0
180
108
1371
518
1758
1356
482
385
6106
4458
Inspectors of Police
Sub-Inspectors of Police
Head Constables
Gr-I Police Constables
Gr-II Police Constables
RANK
Sanctioned
Actual

Fig. 3.

Table 6. Data relating to Women Police in Tamil Nadu.

Sl. No.	Name	Sanctioned Strength	Actual Strength
1.	All Women Police Stations	148	148
2.	Addl. Director Generals of Police	2	2
3.	Inspector Generals of Police	1	1
4.	Deputy Inspector Generals of Police	2	2
5.	Superintendents of Police	4	4
6.	Asst. Superintendents of Police	2	2
7.	Addl. Superintendents of Police	18	18
7.	Deputy Superintendents of Police	12	12
8.	Inspectors of Police	180	108
9.	Sub-Inspectors of Police	1371	518
10.	Head Constables	1758	1356
11.	Police Constables Grade-I	482	385
12.	Police Constables Grade-II	6106	4458

Source: "Hand Book on Police, Tamil Nadu - 2003", Statistical Section, Office of the Director General of Police, Chennai-4.

through the Government's recruitment procedures. Those selected candidates have to be trained before being inducted into the force. This creates a temporary vacuum in the force, but not for long.

The achievements of the All Women Police Stations have become common knowledge by now and their popularity has gained great heights. These stations have provided easier access for women to approach the police for their problems. They have created a forum where the women can discuss their highly personal problems, which they would hesitate to share with the policemen.

Map 1

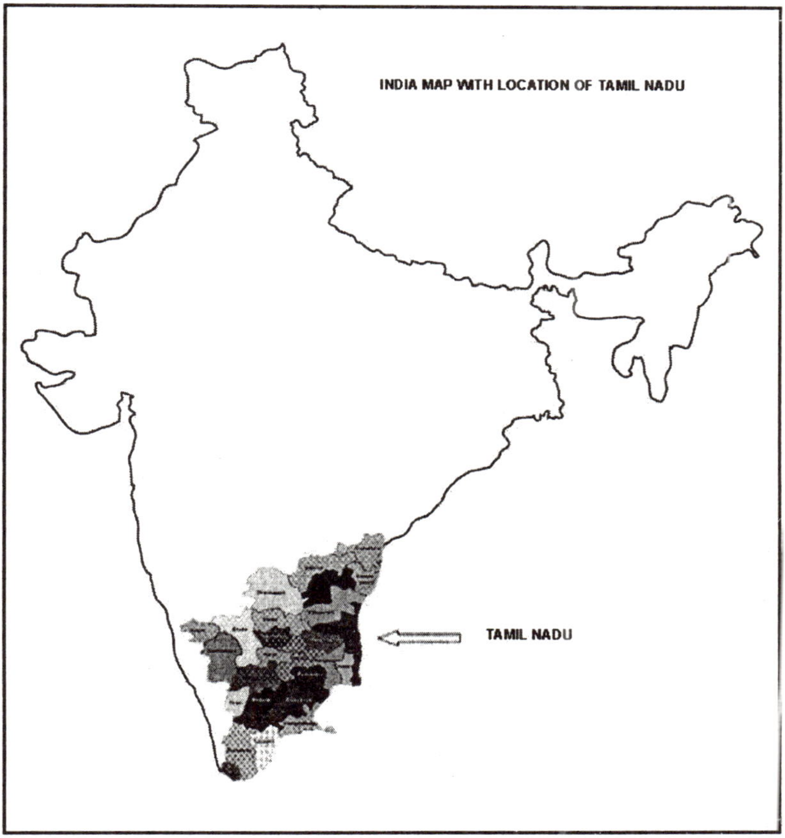

Map 2

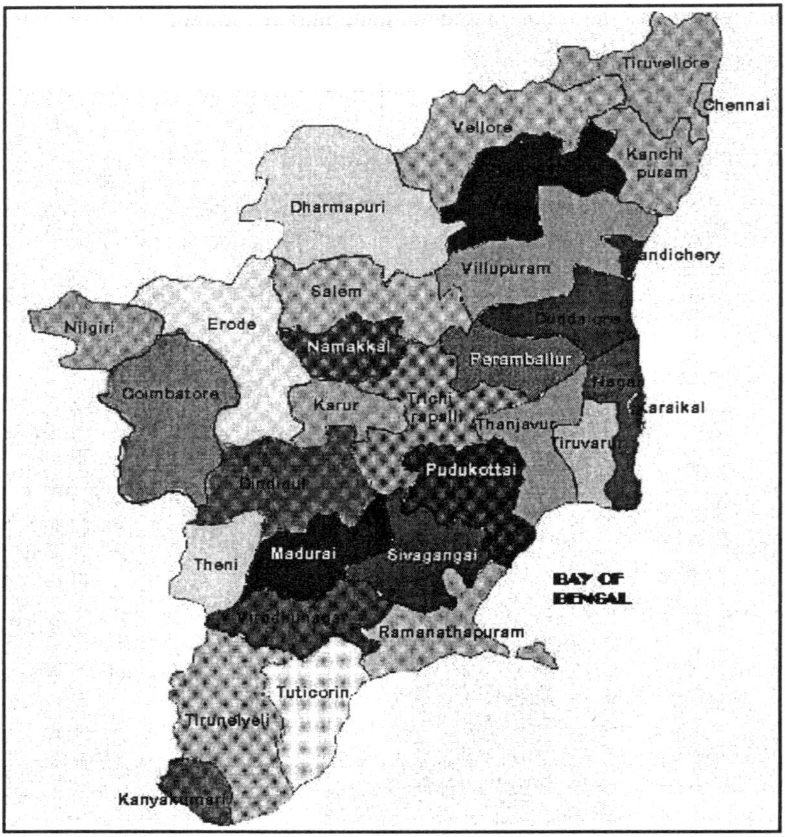
Tiruvellore
Chennai
Vellore
Kanchi
puram
Dharmapuri
Villupuram
Salem
Nilgiri
Erode
Namakkal
Perambalur
Coimbatore
Karur
Trichi
rapalli
Thanjavur
Pudukottai
Theni
Madurai
Sivagangai
BAY OF
BENGAL
Ramanathapuram
Tuticorin
Tirunelveli

Map 3

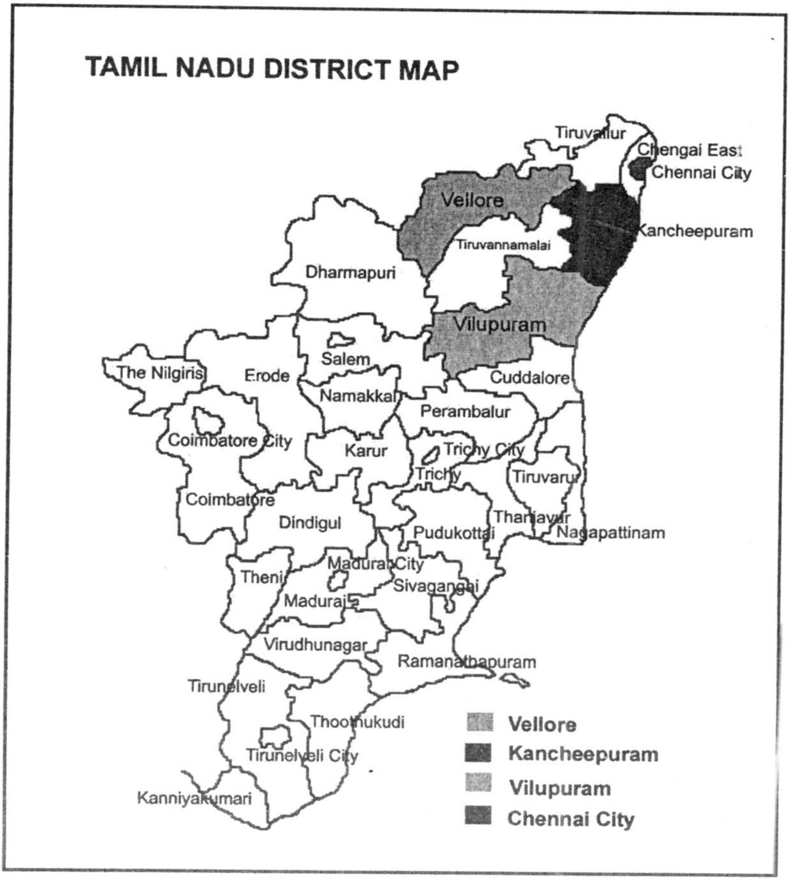
TAMIL NADU DISTRICT MAP
Tiruvallur
Chengai East
Chennai City
Vellore
Kancheepuram
Tiruvannamalai
Dharmapuri
Vilupuram
Salem
The Nilgiris
Erode
Cuddalore
Namakkal
Perambalur
Coimbatore City
Karur
Trichy City
Trichy
Tiruvarur
Coimbatore
Dindigul
Thanjavur
Pudukottai
Nagapattinam
Madurai City
Theni
Sivagangai
Madurai
Virudhunagar
Ramanathapuram
Tirunelveli
Thoothukudi
Tirunelveli City
Kanniyakumari
Vellore
Kancheepuram
Vilupuram
Chennai City

Table 7. Women Police Stations in Tamil Nadu

Sl No.	Cities/District	Sub-Division	Place
1	Chennai City	Flower Bazaar	Kothawal Chavadi
2		Egmore	Thousand Lights
3		Adayar	Adayar
4		Washermenpet	Washermenpet
5		Annanagar	Annanagar
6		Guindy	Ashok Nagar
7		Mambalam	T. Nagar
8		Sembium	Sembium
9		Pulianthope	Pulianthope
10	Coimbatore City	Coimbatore West	R.S. Puram
11		Coimbatore East	Coimbatore East
12		Coimbatore Central	Coimbatore Central
13	Madurai City	Thilagar Thidal	Thilagar Thidal
14		Thallakulam	Thallkulam
15		Madurai Town	Madurai Town
16	Salem City	Salem Town	Salem Town
17		Sooramangalam	Sooramangalam
18		Hasthampatti	Ammapet
19	Trichy City	Fort Range	Fort Range
20		Cantonment	Cantonment
21		Sri rangam	Sir rangam
22	Thirunelveli City	Thirunelveli	Thirunelveli
23		Thirunelveli	Thirunelveli Town
24	Chengalpattu East	St.Thomas Mount	St.Thomas Mount
25		Avadi	Avadi
26		Madipakkam	Neelankarai
27		Ennore	Ennore
28		Poonamalle	Poonamalle

(contd.)

Sl No.	Cities/District	Sub-Division	Place
29	Kancheepuram	Kancheepuram	Kancheepuram
30		Sriperumpudhur	Sriperumpudhur
31		Chengalpattu	Chengalpattu
32		Melmaruvathur	Melmaruvathur
33	Thiruvallur	Thiruthani	Thiruthani
34		Thiruvallur	Thiruvallur
35		Uthukottai	Uthukottai
36	Villupuram	Villupuram	Villupuram
37		Thirukoilore	Thirukoilore
38		Tindivanam	Tindivanam
39		Kallakurichi	Kallakurichi
40		Gingee	Gingee
41	Cuddalore	Cuddalore	Cuddalore
42		Chidambaram	Chidambaram
43		Panrutti	Panrutti
44		Virudhachalam	Virudhachalam
45		Neyveli	Neyveli
46	Vellore	Vellore	Vellore
47		Arakkonam	Arakkonam
48		Tirupathur	Tirupathur
49		Gudiyatham	Gudiyatham
50		Vaniayambadi	Vaniayambadi
51		Ranipet	Ranipet
52		Ambur	Ambur
53	Thiruvannamalai	Thiruvannamalai	Thiruvannamalai
54		T.V. Malai Rural	T.V. Malai Rural
55		Arani	Arani
56		Vandavasi	Vandavasi
57		Polur	Polur

(contd.)

Sl No.	Cities/District	Sub-Division	Place
60		Mettur	Mettur
61		Athur	Athur
62		Omalur	Omalur
63		Sangagri	Sangagri
64	Dharmapuri	Dharmapuri	Dharmapuri
65		Bargur	Bargur
66		Hosur	Hosur
67		Krishnagiri	Krishnagiri
68		Harur	Harur
69		Denkanikottai	Denkanikottai
70	Namakkal	Namakkal	Namakkal
71		Thiruchengode	Thiruchengode
72		Rasipuram	Rasipuram
73	Coimbatore	Thiruppur	Thiruppur
74		Pollachi	Pollachi
75		Udumalaipet	Udumalaipet
76		Pothanur	Pothanur
77		Periyanichenpalayam	Thudiyalur
78		Avinasi	Avinasi
79	Erode	Erode Town	Erode Town
80		Dharapuram	Dharapuram
81		Perundurai	Kangeyam
82		Gobi	Gobichettypalayam
83	The Nilgiris	Ootacamand	Ootacamand
84		Gudalur	Gudalur
85		Coonur	Coonur
86	Trichy	Trichy	Trichy
87		Lalgudi	Lalgudi
88		Musiri	Musiri

(contd.)

Sl No.	Cities/District	Sub-Division	Place
92	Karur	Karur	Karur
93		Kulithalai	Kulithalai
94	Pudukottai	Pudukottai	Pudukottai
95		Aranthangi	Aranthangi
96		Ponnamaravathi	Ponnamaravathi
97		Keeranur	Keeranur
98	Thanjavur	Thanjavur Town	Thanjavur Town
99		Kumbakonam	Kumbakonam
100		Thiruvaiyaru	Thiruvaiyaru
101		Pattukottai	Pattukottai
102		Thanjavur Rural	Papanasam
103	Thiruvarur	Thiruvarur	Thiruvarur
104		Mannarkudi	Mannarkudi
105		Tiruthuraipoondy	Tiruthuraipoondy
106	Nagapattinam	Nagapattinam	Nagapattinam
107		Mayiladuthurai	Mayiladuthurai
108		Sirkazhi	Sirkazhi
109		Vedaraniyam	Vedaraniyam
110	Madurai	Thiruparankundaram	Thiruparankundaram
111		Usilampatti	Usilampatti
112		Melur	Melur
113		Samayanallur	Samayanallur
114	Virudhunagar	Virudhunagar	Virudhunagar
115		Rajapalayam	Rajapalayam
116		Sivakasi	Sivakasi
117		Arupukottai	Arupukottai
118	Dindigul	Dindigul Town	Dindigul Town
119		Palani	Palani
120		Kodaikanal	Kodaikanal

(contd.)

Sl No.	Cities/District	Sub-Division	Place
123	Theni	Theni	Theni
124		Andipatti	Andipatti
125		Bodinaikanur	Bodinaikanur
126	Ramanathapuram	Ramanathapuram	Ramanathapuram
127		Kamudhi	Kamudhi
128		Paramakudi	Paramakudi
129		Keelakarai	Keelakarai
130	Sivagangai	Sivagangai	Sivagangai
131		Karaikudi	Karaikudi
132		Thirupathur	Thirupathur
133		Manamadurai	Manamadurai
134	Thirunelveli	Thenkasi	Thenkasi
135		Valliyur	Valliyur
136		Sankarankoil	Sankarankoil
137		Ambasamuduram	Ambasamuduram
138		Alankulam	Alankulam
139	Thoothukudi	Thoothukudi	Thoothukudi
140		Kovilpatti	Kovilpatti
141		Srivaikundam	Srivaikundam
142		Thiruchendur	Thiruchendur
143		Thoothukudi Rural	Pudukottai
144		Maniyachi	Kadambur
145	Kanniyakumari	Nagercoil	Nagercoil
146		Thakkalai	Thakkalai
147		Kanyakumari	Kanyakumari
148		Colachel	Colachel

Source: "Handbook on Police, Tamil Nadu - 2003", Statistical Section, Office of the Director General of Police, Chennai-4.

The All Women Police Stations are acquiring a qualitatively different character, whereby the nature of problems brought to them has become much more than mere criminal issues. These police stations are gradually turning into centers where a comprehensive approach is brought to bear on women's problems and to solve them by legal as well as counselling techniques.

Need and Significance of the Study

The women police force, in the state of Tamil Nadu was established with the main objective of dealing with women and children. The assumption was that, women possess unique skills and patience and can be expected to deal with women and children with compassion, dignity and respect. Women and children, both, those who are in conflict with law and those in need of protection from victimization, approach the women police. Therefore, there is a felt need to do stocktaking of the performance of the women police in dealing with the above mentioned situations. There is also a need to undertake a scientific research on the evaluation of the performance of the women police in relation to the various tasks assigned to them. It is also required to obtain feed back from the consumers of the services of the women police viz. victims/ complainants, and reflections from the persons who have interacted with the women police namely, the accused and witnesses with regard to their experiences with the women police and perception towards women police. It will also be appropriate to find out factors such as the level of job satisfaction, working conditions, which have influence on the performance of the women police. The outcome of the present research in turn would help to understand the present status of their performance and would also help in identifying the weaknesses/ lacunae, if any, through this research.

The researcher has chosen the sample of his study from the State of Tamil Nadu, which is the Southern most end of India. The State of Tamil Nadu has the largest number of Women Police compared to other states in India. These factors prompted me to select the sample from the state of Tamil Nadu. The concept of All Women Police Stations has been adapted and implemented successfully in this State. So, the researcher took this opportunity to evaluate "The Performance of Women Police in Tamil Nadu" with special reference to Chennai, which is a Corporation and Metropolitan City and adjoining Kancheepuram, Vellore and Villupuram districts, which are having both rural, and town structures. The population of Chennai City is 43.43 lakhs. The Population of Kancheepuram district is 28.77 lakhs. The Population of Vellore district is 34.77 lakhs. The Population of Villupuram district is 29.60 lakhs.

The number of Police Officers versus the number of citizens - 1:778 (Government of Tamil Nadu, Department of Economics and Statistics, Statistical Book-2003)

The changes in social situations with increased association of women in the performance of field duties in several branches of administration and the problems arising out of the increased responsibilities in handling the victims, complainants and witnesses have necessitated the employment of women police officers as such, in a variety of police tasks. It was felt necessary to do a stock-taking of the performance of women police to deal with the victims, complainants and witnesses. There was also a need to undertake a scientific approach on the evaluation of the performance of women police in relation to the various tasks assigned to them. The present study attempts to cover such dimensions, which will have influence on the performance of women police. The outcome of the present research is expected to fill the gap in the existing literature/ studies on women police.

So far the researches were conducted about the formation and functions of women police. Hence it was taken for research to evaluate the performance of women police from the consumer point of view by conducting the present study on the success and failure of the performance of them.

Conclusion

Having realised the need and significance of the problem, it has been proposed to conduct a scientific study on the performance of women police in the State of Tamil Nadu. The researcher has also attempted to review various studies/literatures relating to the present research. The synopsis of such a review has been presented in the next chapter (Chapter 2).

2

Review of Literature

In this chapter, the review of literature related to the present study of performance of Women Police has been presented. The literature based on empirical studies and other articles have been presented according to the key variables chosen for the present study. Though there is enormous literature available on women police, literature based on scientific studies is very limited. This is more true in the Indian context. In India, systematic empirical studies on women police are only few. This may be due to the fact that unlike in developed countries, the origin and development of women police in India is of a recent one. In this context, it is significant to state that the present research will be one of the few scientific studies that have been conducted in India.

The present chapter carries a thorough review of literature related to the present study which includes literature related to performance of women police, their level of job satisfaction, problems faced at their place of work and within the family and society, attitude or perception of victims or public towards women police, treatment of victims or complainants by women police.

Evaluation of the Performance of Women Police

A study on "Female Police Officers: gender bias and professionalism" was conducted, which addressed the differences in perceptions of male and female Police Officers with concern to the appropriateness of action taken on the job, apparent knowledge of Police procedures and their "professionalism" in a certain work situation. For this study a sample of 150 graduate and undergraduate criminal justice students and 44 Police officers rated the Police reports, describing actions taken by an officer during a bank robbery, a drug arrest and a driving-while-intoxicated incident. Contrary to the hypothesis, the reports completed by female officers were consistently scored higher than those completed by male, although most of the differences were not statistically significant. Policewomen were consistently found to be more professional than their male counterparts. Findings also indicated that the perceptions of female police officers can be changed through increased recruitment of women, gender sensitivity training provided at the academies and higher levels of education (Cuadrado, 1996).

Yet another study was conducted to investigate the prevalence of gender differences in the performance of Police applicants on their physical ability tests. In the first phase, data was obtained on the pass or fail rates of 98 female and 743 male applicants belonging to a Mid Western United States police agency from the period of January 1985 to December 1993. In the second phase, questionnaires were completed by 43 of the respondents chosen. The tests had an adverse impact on females and they did not reflect the actual physical tasks that are required for the job (Birzer et al., 1996).

In 2001, a study was conducted among the New York City Police Officers to examine whether gender stereotyped personality traits, function as status–related personality traits. Self-Evaluation Scale (Blascovich and Tomaka, 1991); Police Decision Scale and Unilateral Power and Control Scales. Interviews were conducted with 37 additional officers.

Police Officers' perceptions of their personality traits are determined by status – their individual status vis-a-vis their partner and the group status of their partnership as a whole. The personality traits of men and women also vary according to their status, hence providing support for the status model of gender stereotyping. The personality attributes that are affected by status are the dominating (linked to men) and expressive (linked to women) traits. Higher status police officers of either sex, however, tend to be characterized by more dominating traits in comparison to their partners. By contrast, lower status officers of either sex are characterized by more expressive traits. The partner relationship can influence every aspect of the team's functioning, including how they perceive their personality attributes, their sense of competence, their ability to make decisions and their self-esteem. The organization of the department can further perpetuate sex difference in personality (Gerber, 2001).

In 2001, a study comprising a sample of 185 male and 31 female recruits who were entering the Police

Training Institute at the University of Illinois and who had little or no handgun training was conducted to investigate whether the basic law enforcement firearms class adequately prepared the female officers for this part of their job. Grip strength was measured on the first day of academy attendance and on the last day of the firearms class, using a handgrip dynamometer. For both tests, recruits had to shoot 14 rounds at a paper target from a distance of 15 yards. The firearms training significantly improved the markmanship of all the recruits. Women's scores, however, remained slightly but significantly lower than those of the men's. This small difference appeared to be due to women's lower grip than men's. The findings also suggested that, one way to bring women's skills up to the level of men's, would be to issue the female officers with a weapon, that is suited for their grip strength and hand size. In addition, continued markmanship training that requires additional shooting could not only improve grip strength, but also further enhance their static markmanship scores (Charles and Copay, 2001).

Bartlett and Rosenblum (1977), conducted an 18 month study, during 1976 and 1977 in which 27 policemen and 27 police women, matched for length of service, were compared on 56 performance variables. However, differences were found on only 9. There were no differences in the number or quality of arrests made in any category, the number or quality of other police actions taken, efficiency ratings, injuries, disciplinary charges, the handling of tension or violence, or the attitudes of citizens. Among the differences found were: the policemen were better shots, the policewomen took more sick time, when compared to police men. However the study finally concluded that women were as effective as men in police work.

Homant and Kennedy (1984) conducted a study on "A content analysis of statements about policewomen's handling of domestic violence". This research work looked at 66 statements made by male and female police officers concerning how police women differ in their approach towards family violence cases. The authors argue that the results help document that there are at least two police styles for handling family fighters, and these styles tend to correlate with gender. There is also a significant disagreement, along the gender lines, as to which of these styles is more desirable. The results of this study help to confirm the impression of battered women, that police women had a beneficial impact on them because they were more understanding, showed more concern and provided more information.

Horne (1980) in his study on "Women in law enforcement" concluded that the policewomen do not patrol as well as the policemen. They studied 100 men and 100 women on patrol duties for two years. The report said that the women do not project the impact of strength and power to the same degree as the male officers, and rated the men higher on building searches. Besides, the report also found that women were as diligent as the men in making arrests, with no difference in the number of arrests and rated the women better at handling citizens with guns, family disturbances, and car stops. The report however concluded that women do not handle patrol as safely and efficiently as the men do.

Jefferson et al. (1992) in a study on "Accountability, Control and Social construction of the consumer" has elaborated on the evaluation of police performance which has to be now viewed under a different light. They emphasized that the new ways of thinking about the evaluation of police performance has clearly penetrated the thinking of police managers as they search for consumer evaluation of services. This social construction of the customer has occurred at different rates in different force areas, but is epitomized by the redefinition of police forces as well as Police services. This change of emphasis on the word "service" as opposed to the word "force" draws attention yet again to the question of what constitutes the central policing task.

Linden (1983) in his study found that the performance of women in The Royal Canadian Mount Police appears to be acceptable. Supervisors' evaluation on male and female officers is virtually identical and there is no significant difference in the types of calls handled by men and women. The morale of both male and female officers is quite high, as is the degree of job satisfaction. The major areas of difficulty are higher attrition rates for females and the attitudes of male members towards females (perceived inability of females to handle calls requiring physical strength or force).

Martin (1980), in his study on 'Police women on patrol', showed that many police women do not perform as well as patrol officers. They fall into cycles of failure and demotivation. Lewis (1973) conducted a study on,

'A psychological view of women in policing'. It states that the crime fighting performance of most police women is taken to indicate their inappropriateness for patrol work.

Sherman (1975) in his study on "Evaluation of policewomen on patrol in a suburban police department", observed the policewomen on patrol, in the St. Louis County. This study evaluated the policewomen patrolling alone in a suburban area. The groups evaluated were the first 16 women to be put on patrol in the county, and 16 men who were trained with them. The groups were found to be demographically comparable. The sources of data were observations of patrol, department statistics, interviews and surveys of citizens and department members.

The findings were that the women performed patrol duties as well as the men. They were equally effective in managing distraught or angry citizens. There were no critical incidents, where the policewomen were reported as unable to do their job satisfactorily. The Department's judgment of its own officers showed no difference. Observers made equal ratings of the men and women. The citizens felt that the women were more sensitive and responsive to their needs. The attitudes of the policemen toward the policewomen were mostly negative, although slightly less so after the study.

Sichel et al. (1978) in their study on "Women on Patrol" which was a pilot study of the police performance in New York City made an evaluation that is comparable to the Washington study on the methods of logical sophistication and thoroughness. Forty-one policemen and 41 policewomen were studied for seven months, ending in 1976. The groups were matched for experience - time on the force, time on patrol, type of patrol experience and type of precinct. The study used pairs of observers, one policeman and one civilian, one male and one female, with structured observation forms; interviews with citizens who had contact with the officers; and departmental records and statistics. Over 3,600 hours of patrol were observed, involving 2,400 police-civilian encounters.

In general, the study found that the policemen and policewomen performed similarly. They used the same techniques to gain and keep control. They were equally unlikely to use force or display a weapon. No differences were found in performance, in situations where citizens were agitated or where there were indications of danger; policing style - types of actions taken, interactions with citizens, service orientation, or "calming" effect; self-control, even in extreme cases; activity restraining violent citizens; types of arrests or conviction rates; and performance rating by supervisors. Among the observed differences was that the policemen did more strenuous physical work and were a better option. The policewomen made fewer arrests and took more sick time.

Peter et al. (1974), conducted a study on police women on patrol. The study shows that sex is not a bonafide occupational qualification for doing patrol work. Van Wormer (1981) in his article entitled "Are Males suited to Police Patrol Work?" said that policemen are more prone to violence and of unbecoming conduct. They overprotect police women and, then complain that they were a handicap. Policewomen meet the public better. They are better at dealing with rape victims and handling domestic violence. He further suggested that the shortcomings of male officers could possibly be overcome by special selection and training.

In a paper presented by Balkin (1988) on "Why Policemen don't like Police women" which was carried out by conducting a case study on 86 newly trained policemen and 86 newly trained police women", revealed the contrast in their experience and general background such as education and civil test score. The findings also revealed that men and women performed patrol work in the same manner, responded to similar calls such as the women making fewer arrests and issuing fewer traffic tickets. The findings also projected the difference in their policing style, by which it was found that though the policemen and women were both equally effective in handling any incident, the male officers remained convinced in their biased opinion that men were better rated than police women especially in handling violent situations and competency.

Literature Relating to Job Satisfaction

In a study on "Various aspects of discrimination in the police" particularly in the region of England and Wales conducted by Anderson et al. (1993) pointed out that the deployment patterns of women police officers gravitated towards "low frequency", for example supportive for women. It was also found that policewomen were under-represented in many specialist departments and totally absent from others. These observations were supported by others like Holdaway and Parker (1998) in their studies. Hence Anderson et al. concluded that as a consequence, women officers were limited in the amount and type of experience they were able to gain. This in turn affects their job satisfaction and may inhibit their promotion prospects. Finally, they emphasized that fewer women than men achieve promotion, which in turn can reinforce male stereotypes about women's abilities.

Brown et al. (1995), in their study on "Police Women and firearms in the British Police Service" found that only 6% of the United Kingdom's officers are authorized to carry firearms. The study examines the reasons why male and female officers volunteer for, or are not interested in, being trained for firearm duties. Questionnaires were completed by 4 samples: 715 male and female constables; a follow-up with 448 constables; 99 officers currently authorized to carry firearms; and 84 officers recently resigned from firearm duties. There was a higher than expected rate of interest with respect to firearm duties, expressed by women police officers. The most frequent reason offered for volunteering was the belief that it would bring greater variety to their jobs; this finding may reflect some job dissatisfaction of the police women. Men revealed some resistance toward having women serve as firearm officers, believing that they do not possess appropriate qualities.

A study conducted by Holdaway and Parker (1998) in Northern England, examines female officers' experience of the police department. Data were obtained from questionnaires completed by female (N=263) and male (N=320) officers serving in a Northern England constabulary, as well as focus groups and selective interviews with senior officers. It was deduced from the study that the work of women officers was constrained by societal structures of gendered inequalities. Conflicts between work and parental responsibilities for example were generally sharper for women officers.

Though many features of the occupational culture of the rank and file were discriminatory, women officers sustained key features of that culture, mostly by placing and retaining aspects of crime work in the ascendancy. Though many features in the working atmosphere of the officers and colleagues were discriminatory, the women officer stood such factors of discrimination and proved their efficiency in crime work. Though the crime investigation division was a particular enclave of discriminatory and exclusionary practices, many women chose to apply to join the Criminal Investigation Department. Thus, female officers in some ways reinforced the dominant assumptions about police work espoused by their male colleagues and in other ways they sought to overcome their marginalization within the work force.

Dantzker et al. (1998) conducted a study on "Job satisfaction: the gender perceptive among Police Officers". The study examined the effect of gender on job satisfaction among Police Officers. Data were obtained from questionnaires completed by 2,390 male and 309 female officers in 7 states of the United States of America. In general, the study concluded that female officers had similar levels of job satisfaction as male officers.

Simpson (1977), Fagerstrom (1970) and Sherman (1973) conducted similar studies and concluded that the police departments throughout the United States of America had policies that discouraged the hiring of women, including quotas, usually one percent or less. The work of policewomen tended to be restricted to cases involving women and children and for clerical duties. In most police departments, the prevailing feeling was that women were not fit for regular police work.

With reference to their study in "Sources of stress among women police officers ", Wexler and Logan (1983) interviewed the California Patrol officers. They concluded that women were not more dissatisfied than men with tasks or administrators, nor with the impact of their jobs on family life. But they also revealed that women uniformly saw sexist attitudes of colleagues as significant sources of stress; not surprisingly, men did not report sexism as stressful.

More subjects presently in the all women units preferred an integrated role and department style than in 1994. In addition, many more new recruits in comparison to the officers in the All-female units wished to be fully integrated. More of the recruits, in turn, wanted to be fully integrated in comparison to those interviewed in 1988. Despite the trend toward fuller integration, the aspirations of the new recruits lagged far behind those of their counterparts in the United States. On the other hand, they did not seem very different from the performance of police women in Europe.

Literature relating to Problems Faced by the Women Police at workplace

A study on "Aspects of discriminatory treatment of women police officers serving in forces in England and Wales" was conducted by Brown (1998). This study examined discriminatory treatment of female police officers in England and Wales. Data on women officers' operational tasks, access to deployment and promotional opportunities and exposure to sexual harassment were obtained from: (1) a secondary analysis of official 1990 data on officers in 42 of the United Kingdom Police forces; and (2) questionnaires completed in 1992 by 1,802 female officers and 510 male constables in London and 5 provincial agencies; and (3) questionnaires completed by 164 female civilian personnel employed at 2 police forces.

The study deduced that women were still under represented both laterally and horizontally in the Police service. Discriminatory and harassing behaviour occurred frequently. The working environment could not be changed merely by the necessity for equal opportunities and other policy initiatives over the last 20 year. Thus, further deconstruction of the police occupational culture and the obstacles it poses for women in the police service are warranted.

To examine the social organizational relationships and interactions that positions the African American police women as outsiders within their own department, a research study was under taken. Data were obtained from semi-structured interviews with all 21 black females from a force of approximately 1400 sworn law enforcement officers working in an urban police department in the United States. The median age of the women was 37 years. Their police employment ranged from 1 to 22 years. Their educational background varied from high school to postgraduate degrees, with more than half having attended or graduated from college. The women often experienced gender discrimination related to professional abilities, job performance and supervisory responsibilities. They also experienced racism in the form of derogatory remarks and in the areas of hiring and promotion. Their exclusion arises not only from dominant white men but from other subordinated groups such as white female and black male officers (Pogrebin et al. 2000.

Slonaker et al. (2001) examined employment discrimination claims filed by police officers and applicants for officer jobs between 1985 and 1999. Data on 79 such claims were derived from a continuing longitudinal study of employment discrimination claims closed by the Ohio Civil Rights Commission (OCRC) during this period.

Male officers most frequently (34%) cited race as the basis for discrimination, whereas female officers most often (65%) based their claims on sex. Other precipitators were: not being hired, being unfairly disciplined, being terminated, not being promoted, being harassed, and not receiving pay and benefits. For the claims made by officers, or those who were denied employment as such, the outcomes were as follows: (a) No probable cause was found in 18% of the cases, (b) the claims were settled by the employer and officer in 15% of the claims, (c) probable cause was found in just 2 of the claims, and (d) 1 claimant withdrew her claim early to obtain her right-to-sue letter and to file a suit in court without awaiting the outcome of the OCRC's investigation.

In a study conducted by Flynn (1982) on the gender based differences among police officers, it was found that the gender based differences among police officers are significant for at least two reasons. First, to the extent that women routinely experience exclusion, discrimination and hostility from their male supervisors and colleagues, their attitudes toward work- their satisfaction, commitment, integration and aspirations - may be severely compromised. Second, the presumption that women and men have fundamentally different priorities and perspectives on human relationships underlies some observer's arguments for greater integration of women into the police departments (and into the criminal justice system more generally).

The review of the role, status and character of police women in Africa by Igbinovia (1987) states that, historically, women have been discriminated against in their desire to join the African police forces. Few African police services are now employing women, and those who are employed perform as generalists, working with minors and children, and are not entrusted with actual police power and authority. This has been so in spite of the evidence that police women perform as well as policemen in police work assignments. The author recommends greater employment of women in the police departments and broadening of their present role.

Johns (1979) studied criminal justice students, and found that a majority of the men felt that women are not suited for patrol, or none at all. This study, aside from its pessimistic implications, suggested that attitudes about policewomen come not from observation and experience but from persisting attitudes and values.

Yang (1985) in his study on "Women in policing" where he has compared the United States and China and made an exploratory effort to identify similarities/ dissimilarities in policewomen's role in the United States and the Republic of China (Taiwan) and analyze them in the historical, cultural and structural contents of these two countries.

The conclusions suggested that the policies relating to police personnel in the United States are mainly determined and administered by the individual police departments, where as in the Republic of China, a nationally centralized police authority mandates the regularity of these personnel practices. Also, the discriminatory practices against policewomen have induced more attention from the public and more consciousness among the women themselves in the U.S. than in the Republic of China. Also, since the American policewomen have been more self-conscious of their inferior status and more active in fighting for equality, they inevitably pose a greater threat to their male counterparts, thus arousing more hostility and opposition. In the Republic of China, on the other hand, females have not been able to constitute any potential threat to the males in law enforcement, and hence, have not experienced strong negative feelings against them.

Wyles (1952) conducted a study on "Women at Scotland Yard." It showed that generally women police officers in sharp contrast to their male colleagues believed that they are discriminated against, that police men are prejudiced against them, that they greatly over emphasize the importance of physical strength in the job – that women are effectively excluded from some of the more interesting kinds of work and that men will not accept them as full members of the working group or as colleagues on an equal basis.

Lehtinen (1976) has summed up the women's situation by observing that they are fighting injustice within the police department more than on the streets. 'The only trouble with women in policing is men in policing' .

In the year 1988, a survey was conducted among 541 female Police Officers in the United States of America and obtained names from the Executive Directors of 4 state Peace Officers Standards and Training (POST) academies. Responses were received from 9 western states. The findings of the study revealed that open sex discrimination and sexual harassment were more common than supposed - particularly by supervisors and commanders, who not only tolerated such practices by others but were frequently perpetrators themselves. Most respondents did not think that sex should be an issue in the assignment of duties to an officer, though in practice it was. Few gave men or women any particular "edge" in law enforcement. The majority were well trained, had 6 or more years of experience (mostly in patrol), were well-paid and enjoyed their profession. The overall pattern of responses suggested that law enforcement has a long way to go in equal employment opportunity and fair employment practices (Timmins and Hainsworth, 1989).

The studies conducted by Horne (1980) on department attitudes, generally showed that most chiefs as well as male officers hold unfavourable attitudes, sometimes even distrustful ones, towards policewomen. These attitudes are by all means discernable in various formal practices (e.g., assignment, promotion) and informal interactions (e.g., Languages, sexual attitudes).

Sullivans interpersonal theory (1953) "discusses the anxiety associated with women police who undermine the male officers perception of his masculinity by their very presence. The women do their work perhaps not with equal physical strength, but with equal courage and competence. If the male police officer recognises the worth of them, it would make him feel less manly, so he distorts his views of them to perceive them as not strong, competent/courageous. His male colleagues maintain their own distorted views for the same reasons, so they collectively reinforce these distorted views. When women move into previously male dominated work, and 'shock, horror' do it well, it challenges the males' perception of his self worth. He feels, that a woman doing his traditional tasks, devalues him as a man.

The findings of the study conducted by Krishnamurthi (1995) on "Women Police in criminal justice administration" indicated that in the area of traditional role performance, the respondents playing the role of mother and/or single parent experienced higher role conflict and tension as compared to their performance in other familial roles such as wife and daughter. Women police were found to be in greater degree of tension in areas relating to inadequacies of managing time, energy and resources. In the job related areas, higher tension and conflict was due to the type of duty allotted to them rather than the relationship or attitude of their counterparts either male or female.

Chakravarthy (1994) in his study "Equal opportunities to Women in Police" deduced on the fact that, more women entering the police force, has become responsible for considerable reduction in the use of third degree methods and with better training and knowledge of the law, women can safeguard themselves from sexual harassment by their superiors. He also elucidated that a strong disciplinary support from the higher ups could eliminate the non- cooperation from male subordinates in the force.

Literature Relating to Problems Faced by the Women Police within the Family and Society

Elliot and Frazer (1986) carried out a study, to determine the relationship among marital intimacy, marital satisfaction and police officers. A sample of practicing officers and their spouses were interviewed. The findings of the study showed that: marital satisfaction among police officers is relatively unaffected by life stress; marital intimacy does not serve as a mediating variable to police officers' stress; wives' marital satisfaction is more adversely affected by insufficient or excessive marital intimacy than in the husbands.

Janus et al. (1988) in their paper examined the views of women regarding their femininity and changes in their social life and work as a result of being sworn as police officers. A questionnaire provided information on demographics, personal factors, work experience, attitudes towards femininity, police work, life-styles, male officers, family and partners. The paper examined both the self-image and the functional aspects of the lives of women in police work. The sample population for this study consisted of 135 women, all of whom are full time sworn police officers. Their ages ranged from 21-52, and they have served as full time police from one to 28 years. Most women are comfortable with their roles and in fact an overwhelming number reported feeling more comfortable with male officers. There seems to be no loss of feminine identity as a result of being a police officer and many responses indicated that being a woman has been an asset in police work.

Family support is seen as being important in the choice of police work, these women have made. Lovers and social life did not suffer at all from the nature of the work, the respondents were engaged in, or the roles these women played. The only issue raised that interfered with their social lives was the time scheduling in their work lives.

Taylor (1974) conducted a study on "Women Police Officers and their husbands". The study revealed that policemen usually keep wives out of their professional lives. The divorce rate among cops has always been high.

Attitude/Perception of Women Police Towards Policing and Working Conditions

Charles (1982) in his study on "Women in Policing: the Physical Aspect", states that traditionally it has been the opinion of many police personnel that women are not physically, not to mention psychologically or emotionally, strong enough to meet the demands of the police profession. Evidence suggests that this perception is incorrect. While women generally may not be as physically strong as men, they may train themselves to achieve a level of fitness well within the normal demands of the profession.

Davis (1984) conducted a study on "Perspectives of the policewomen" in Texas and Oklahoma. The focus of the study was a comparison of male and female perspectives in policing within a sequence of four topic areas. These included perspectives on social causation, enforcement, stress, and professional self-assessments.

The findings tallied with the previous researches in some instances, and in some it did not and suggested new conclusions in yet others. Quite unlike previous researches, the policewomen were found to be more authoritarian than the policemen. They also appeared to be more cynical about human nature as it affects obedience to law. Despite the evidence in the literature of fewer arrests by policewomen, this research found little difference in the predispositions towards arrest of male and female officers. However, the policewomen were significantly more inclined to intervene when infractions were observed. Together these predispositions towards arrest and intervention suggest, along with other research, that the females may be more flexible than the males in their approach to enforcement.

Hester et al. (1988) studied the personality and attitudes of the female police officers. The results indicated that the recruits rated themselves as higher on masculine traits without rating themselves as less feminine.

Pinto (1988) conducted a study on "Police women's perception of their changing role". The research examined, the role of women in the Victoria (Australia) Police force in terms of their deployment and career prospects, the attitudes of respondents towards the present and preferred roles of the policewomen and determined, whether "informal barriers" exist as a result of adverse male attitudes. The survey's findings indicated that policewomen overwhelmingly preferred to occupy the same role as that which is occupied by policemen. Despite these preferences, however, the study found that policewomen believed that supervisory officers often deploy the policewomen on different duties than they do the policemen. The results also indicated that the respondents believed that the policemen displayed negative attitudes towards the policewomen performing the same duties that they do. The policewomen generally feel that they have equal opportunities for promotion as the policemen and they are not discriminated against, because of their sex. A significant proportion of respondents believed that it is difficult to combine policing with marriage and the family. Respondents who commenced duties prior to the introduction of Equal opportunity legislation generally felt that the legislation positively affected the role of women in policing.

Worden (1993), in his study on "The attitudes of women and men in policing", examined the conflicting predictions about gender and attitudes derived from theory about occupational socialization, drawing upon the former to develop hypotheses about four dimensions of police attitudes: perspectives on the police role, attitudes toward citizens, evaluation of departments and co-workers and occupational integration. These hypotheses were tested with the data obtained from the police service study, which surveyed police officers in 24 departments. The results suggest that although men and women may not be equally integrated into their jobs as police officers, there are few differences in the ways men and women see their role, their clientele or their departments.

A study on "Women Police in a traditional society" was conducted by Natarajan (2001). The study examined the contention that female police officers in traditional societies do not aspire to full integration into mainstream policing but instead may prefer a more restricted and segregated role. Policing in Tamil Nadu, a state in India, is analysed using data from: interviews with 75 female officers, questionnaires completed by 140 officers (including the preceding 75) and visits to 6 battalions where new recruits were assigned, during which interviews were conducted with an additional 55 officers and questionnaires completed by 104 individuals. Comparisons were made with additional groups of female officers: (a) 61 officers in all women police units in Tamil Nadu in 1994 (b) 183 officers in Tamil Nadu in 1988 (before the establishment of all women units) and (c) 196 officers in New Jersey in 1988.

Natarajan (2001) has conducted a study on "Women Police in a Traditional Society" - a different angle of study from that of the present researcher by way of evaluating the performance of women police by examining accused, victims, witnesses and women police themselves about their job satisfaction.

Chakravarthy (1994) in his study "Equal opportunities to Women in Police" also emphasized that a clear understanding and complete preparedness on the part of the spouses, provision of residential quarters at the place of posting and a break for 2-3 years without pay to sort out domestic issues can help the women in the police force to thwart any attempt on character assassination and tide over the situations arising from their separation from husband and family.

Attitude/Perception of Victims/ Public towards Women Police

The studies reviewed by Charles and Parsons (1978) on 'Female performance in the law enforcement function' to determine the public attitude towards women police revealed that the American citizens generally hold positive opinions about female police officers and often describe them as more sympathetic, empathic, compassionate and better in handling service calls and domestic quarrels than the male officers. In addition, the females seem to be more effective in avoiding violence under potentially violent circumstances.

Similarly, Hanmer and Saunders (1991) presented a paper in "Policing violence against women" during the British Criminology Conference in 1991, which revealed that the employment of women officers is an issue both in relation to requests by women and agencies in the community for women officers and also the transformation of masculine police culture in order to provide a more satisfactory service for women. They also stated that the appointment and promotion of women police still remains an issue. Women in the West Yorkshire police constituted only 9 per cent of the force in November 1987 when the earlier research was completed. This rose to 13.5 per cent in 1991. However, 13.5 per cent of the senior officers were not women. Their studies also revealed that inadequate numbers of women officers and their position in the force continues to be commented upon by other agencies, but the force's response to this recommendation was to describe themselves as an equal opportunity employer.

Bell (1982) described a study of the police chiefs supervising policewomen in 42 major U.S. cities. Seventy per cent of them felt that policewomen, properly trained, were as good as policemen. But, Bell also cited certain other studies in which the supervising officer contradictorily felt that the policewomen were weak, undependable, and not suited for general patrol work.

Joyce et al. (1977) conducted a study on 'Women on patrol' which showed that despite the fact that the male and female officers performed similar duties and used the same techniques to gain and maintain control, the female officers were judged by civilians to be more competent, pleasant, respectful and understanding than their male counterparts.

Kennedy and Homant (1983) in their study on "Attitudes of abused women toward male and female police officers" found that policewomen were especially valued in domestic disputes. It was felt that policewomen were able to calm down an angry man, understand him and prevent violence. Most important was the policewoman's ability to show concern.

A survey conducted by Radford (1987) on "Women policing and male violence" revealed that 44 per cent of the samples chosen, thought that women officers would be more understanding in relation to violence against women, though 32 per cent thought they would not be. Many said that they would prefer to speak to women in the context of domestic violence but similarly others recognized that women officers had to be tougher than the men to succeed.

Austin and Hummer (1999) conducted a study on "what do college students think of Police Women?". It was carried out to find out the attitudes toward women in the field of policing among 835 under graduate students enrolled at a North Eastern United States University. It was found that attitudes of male college students in general and those of male criminal justice majors in particular, towards women as Police Officers were somewhat negative, though they have shown a significant degree of change over the past decade. Female students, regardless of their major area of study, remain quite positive on the idea in law enforcement. Having a family member in law enforcement was significant for approximately half the attitudinal and semantic differential items: respondents with such a relative were less supportive of policewomen than those without a family member working in the field.

Walklate (1992) has spoken on "Responding to domestic violence" at the University of Salford. While comparing the policewomen with policemen, she stated that the moral behaviour of the women concerned is much more likely to be subjected to scrutiny than of their male counterparts. Such public perception and expectations constitute the background against which, more specific experience of police women are to be evaluated or understood. The dilemma tend to exist at a personal level in the tension between police women's task of arresting the perpetrator and the demands of their role in supporting the affected women. In one of the training sessions conducted for officers (99% female and all constables) the feedback received was a wholehearted urge to be listened to and to be given their due place while expressing their views within their own organization.

A study by Sutton (1996) on "Women in Policing" emphasizes the need for outstanding women officers to be encouraged to get involved in education and training roles both at the academy and in the field, which would put up role models for female police to look up to and take up. She also suggested that in order to deal with a situation such as domestic violence and dowry death (a) at least 25% of the police force should consist of women police. (b) More women police stations should be opened in all states.

The increase in the number of women in the force is also desirable in order to deal with women agitators and offences against women.

Aleem (1991b) also conducted a study on 'Women Police' in the year 1991. In her study, an attempt was made to study the peoples' perception on the role of women police in India. The focus of the study was more on the functions and role of women police. The results indicate that in general, people do not have a very high opinion of the women police but they are confident that if given an opportunity, the women police can act as an instrument of social change and do well.

With reference to the role of women police in criminal justice administration, Krishnamurthi (1996) is of the view that even though the status of women in the police, of late, has been considered indispensable, still the use of their potentialities is inadequate, sidelined and stagnant. It is almost a hundred years since women entered the police field but even then, they are not considered equal to their male counterparts. Krishnamurthi further suggests that the women police should be involved on a priority basis in all the functions concerning women. A proper understanding and realization of the roles and status of the women police in criminal justice system will enable them to excel in the police job. A similar view was also expressed by Mahajan (1982). He said that women's role in policing remains ambiguous due to organizational apathy, opposition from the male incumbents, negative societal reaction, lack of committed police women and lack of opportunities for women to occupy positions of authority in the police organizations.

Treatment of the Victims/Complainants by the Women Police

A study was carried out to investigate how female and male police officers perceive and respond to a hypothetical but realistic domestic violence situation in the North Georgia area of the United States. Subjects (female officers-40 and male officers-214) were drawn from public safety training centers responsible for providing in-service training to experienced officers and mandatory training to rookie officers in the North Georgia area. Each officer was randomly assigned to read 1 of 12 scripts in which 3 features of the domestic violence situation were manipulated: the wife's conduct (normal, hallucinating, drunken); the presence of visible injuries on the wife; and antagonism between wife and husband. Female and male officers did not differ on arrest rates; however, women officers were more likely to recommend shelters and less likely to advise marriage counseling. These gender differences occurred only among experienced female officers. Women also assigned more importance to the victims' willingness to settle the argument in their arrest decisions. Based on these findings, it appears that female police officers will increase battered women's satisfaction with how officers handle their cases. Female officers, compared to males, were likely to provide victims with more information and would increase rates of referrals to shelters, but will not generate higher arrest rates (Stalans and Finn, 2000).

Prussel and Lonsway (2001) in their study projected the benefits of hiring and retaining female police officers and provide guidance for agencies seeking to evaluate their own recruitment policies and procedures. Compared with men, women more often use a communicative style consistent with the principles of community policing and are substantially less likely to use excessive force, respond more sympathetically to violent crime victims and provide an impetus for "family-friendly" and other policies. Among the many ways of recruiting female officers, are paid advertising career fairs and the Internet. Also recommended are regional training seminars and self-assessment guides available from the National Criminal Justice Reference Service.

Lonsway et al. (2001) in a round table discussion, conducted at the Sixth Annual Conference of the National Center for Women and Policing, seven academics and practitioners focus on the use of force among female police officers. The research clearly indicates that, although men and women are equally likely to use force in their routine duties as law enforcement officers, women are less likely to engage in excessive force. Instead, women officers tend to emphasize communication and de-escalation of potentially violent situations, a style that is more in line with community policing ideals. Progressive institutions, such as the New Haven (Connecticut) Police Department demonstrate that these skills can be taught at the academy and the new officers can be integrated into the communities in which they serve.

Studies/Literature in General on Women Police

Belknap and Douglas (1994) conducted a study on "Woman battering and Police referrals". The study examines the use of referrals by the police in woman battering cases and the officers' characteristics associated with these referrals. A sample of about 324 law enforcement officers in a large United States Midwestern metropolitan area were chosen who completed questionnaires in December 1987.

Almost three fourth of the officers reported as providing referrals in battering cases, most often to a women's victim hotline and organization. However, the officer's gender and socio-economic status were not related to their responses, but it was found that highly educated officers provided more referrals. The most important predictor of reported referral behaviour was departmental affiliation: the more conservative the department was, the more likely it was to have officers making referrals to Alcoholics Anonymous and public welfare agencies, as well as both religious and non-religious counselling. Improved officer training and policy guidelines could encourage the wider and more consistent use of referrals.

Chesshyre (1989) in his article 'Softly Softly' talks about policewomen and says that although their numbers are not yet adequately or fairly reflected in crucial areas like crime - fighting and firearms, women officers are beginning to add integrity to the prevailing police force. Male chauvinism and chivalry can keep them off frontline duty, yet they have the skills to talk their way convincingly through the most confrontational situations. The prejudice faced by policewomen is not confined to their male colleagues. The public instinctively feels that a policeman must be more effective than a female counterpart. The next few years will bring not just more women police, but, for the first time, a significant wedge of influential senior women whose perception of policing is likely to lean more towards the notion of 'service than of force'. Women will have to be exceptionally good to succeed.

Garrison et al. (1988) conducted a study on 'Utilization of police women'. This study reports the results of an initial national survey in the United States of the police women and a review of the literature assessing the degree of current utilization of females in law enforcement. The literature suggests that women made limited gains in hiring and in career opportunities in law enforcement during the late 1970s and early

1980s. According to the latest available data, more policewomen were in non-traditional jobs than ever before, but they were not the majority of female personnel. There is no reason to believe that time alone will rectify the liased use of women across police functions. Survey instruments were completed by 180 members of the International Association of Police Women. With the exception of opportunities for special training, less than half the sample thought they were utilized properly, used their skill or had the same assignment opportunities as men.

Heidensohn (1992) from her study on "Role and control of Women in Law Enforcement" in the year 1992, suggested certain levels of satisfaction and support which are maintained for both the women being supported and police women themselves when they are involved in this kind of work. However, Heidensohn from her interviews also deduced that the possession of sympathetic listening skills are not necessarily associated with women. Finally, she was able to conclude that, it is the innate quality that is embedded in their nature, to act with ease that has placed them as workers within the male dominated profession.

Jones (1986) conducted a study on "Policewomen and Equality". In the examination of the impact that the Sex Determination Act (1975) has had on the current role of women in the police service in Great Britain. The book examined the experiences of men and women who joined the police service both before and after the Act, which in theory should have led to full equality for women with their male colleagues. By comparing the recruitment, deployment and career experiences of men and women and the attitudes of both male and female officers toward the present and preferred roles of policewomen, the author examines formal equal opportunity policy and the reality of policewomen's working lives. What is clear from this analysis is that the behaviour prescribed by the equal opportunities legislation is not reflected in the attitudes of the majority of policemen and that, in reality, informal practices which more closely follow these attitudes have a major impact on the working lives of policewomen. In conclusion, the author considers institutional working solutions that would limit the development and continuation of informal practice: the formulation and implementation of equal opportunities policy, management and supervision procedures, and organizational provisions designed to enable women officers to develop their careers.

Warner et al. (1989) conducted a study to examine the conditions of society with progress towards increasing the number of women employees in police and analyzed data from surveys of 281 of the United States of American City Police Departments in 1984 and 1987. The variation among cities in employment of female police officers is probably due to a combination of economic conditions, local-level representation of women in public offices and explicit administrative mechanisms established for hiring women. Progress toward social equality for women in such male-dominated occupations as policing is highly dependent on a formal administrative structure, established specifically to achieve this goal.

Wimshurst (1995), in a study investigated the large-scale entry of women into Queensland (Australia) Policing, survey data were obtained in 1992 and 1993 from 91 male and 44 female recruits. The findings of the study revealed that continuity rather than change is likely to characterize the experiences of women entering policing; obstacles to full integration persist. One example is the continuing powerful influence of the cult of physicality in defining police work. Media reports tend to portray female officers in a trivial or deviant light. The number of women in senior ranks remains extremely low; thus female role models for the influx of new recruits are few and far between. Female officers must become more assertive in developing political and professional strategies to further their own interests.

In 1994, a qualitative study on the problems and experiences of Police women in Spain was conducted. Data from 5 life-histories and a focus group were analyzed on: organizational control of police women; the motivation of women to pursue a career in the criminal justice system; relationships with their families; specific problems of police women; and other topics (Fernandez, 1994).

Martin (1999) reviewed the feelings and display rules that regulate emotional expression in police work, the ways these are made masculine and how this affects occupational and organizational norms. Variations are identified in the norms regulating emotional labour across policing assignments, situations, and gender of both the officer and the citizen in an encounter. Coping mechanisms for regulating emotions - socialization, organizational rituals, humor and off-duty social activities - are explored, as is the dilemma that norms related to emotional labour pose for women officers.

Jeanne and Richard (2001) carried out research on "Police work in the Caribbean: The influence of gender and nation". This qualitative study of gender across socio-political contexts assesses the applicability of models constructed in the United States and the United Kingdom to Caribbean nations. Survey data were collected from 1,237 police constables and immediate supervisors in Barbados, Trinidad and Tobago and Jamaica. Questions were based on 24 constructs evaluated in the American and British literature. A total of 11% of respondents were women. Perceptions of the policing experience are shaped more by the nation within which the force is located than by the gender of the constable. Thus, women officers appeared to have more in common with their male colleagues than they did with female constables in other nearby nations. In addition, a nation's level of gender equality did not seem to differentially affect the perceptions of women and men constables. Future studies should pay attention to more macro-level factors specific to each nation's police organization and administration.

Dick and Jankowicz (2001), in their study identified the values that configure the police culture and examined whether men and women articulated similar values. Data consisted of interviews with one United Kingdom Police force, conducted from October 1993 to April 1999 (N=51). Overall, memberships of a supervisory rank, rather than gender, has the greatest influence on the content of officers' performance value judgements. In particular, constables, as the most subordinate rank, are motivated to emphasize the vocational, mission-like aspects of the police role. Being in a position of power, however, as the supervisory ranks are, exposes cynical discourses that are circulated by the lower ranks. Gender does have some influence on the way knowledge is constructed, but this is better understood as being related to socio-cultural constructions of gender identity rather than to any essential characteristics of men and women per se. As opposed to creating more women friendly policies such as job-share and part-time working, police organization should focus on practices such as long working hours, staying behind after a shift to deal with a prisoner and shift-work in general.

Hearn (1987) in his study on "Gender of Oppression" stated that those police parts of the state are found to be fully male dominated and male membered which are more concerned with violence and repression than those parts which are concerned with caring, welfare and reproduction.

In a study of "Police Women in the news" by Soothill (1993), it has been stated that a close examination of the various images of policing only reveals that those images only presume a male police officer, whereas the images of female police officers are very few. Soothill in his study also pointed out that how surprisingly the newspaper coverage of police women without being biased, focus on traditionally stereotypical areas for women and at the same time there is also a coverage of police women and their role in more dangerous activities of police work.

Dorothy Smith (1990) in her lecture at the 25th Conference of Canadian Learned Societies, metaphorises the role of women in police to the old Lancashire saying of "Whistling Women and a crowning hen, let the devil out of his pen". She projects that this saying draws our attention to the powerful effect anomalies can have. Pointing out to the example of Alison Halford as one such anomaly, she states that apart from being a powerful policewoman she was also a difficult enough combination for a male membered police organization.

Woolf (1967) in her book "A Room of Ones Own" points out towards the hostile behaviour of men towards the role of police women, especially when they wish to enlarge the boundaries to take in the traditional male roles. She states that "Women have served all these centuries as looking glasses possessing the magic and delicious power of reflecting the figure of man at twice its actual size". In other words she emphasizes that men hate women because they need women to define their selfimage.

An examination of factors that affected the hiring of female police officers by municipal police officers in the United States was carried out as a separate study. From the study, it was found that affirmative action litigation significantly increased the hiring of new female recruits, but female political representation in the form of female city councilors or mayors did not significantly affect the gender composition of Police recruits. Consistent with co-worker discrimination, the hiring of female recruits was negatively related to the proportion of males already employed in the department. Male-dominated departments were also more likely to employ fitness examinations for recruits (a potential barrier to women) than more integrated departments. The effect of police union was mixed, there was some evidence that unions boosted the hiring of female officers, yet unions were also associated with an increased likelihood of using fitness examinations to screen new recruits (Tim and Jennifer, 1999).

Rao et al. (1975) conducted a study on "Women Police in India", with the object of reviewing the growth and development of women police in India. The study also examined the organizational structure and its units. Further, the authors also analyzed their functions and role in various fields of operations and attempted to provide broad guidelines for organizational growth and development. Regarding the need for a growth and expansion of women police in the State of Jammu and Kashmir, Singh (1984) said that the total strength of women police in Jammu and Kashmir is more than one hundred. As the state of crime is rising in Jammu and Kashmir, there is a need for planned growth and expansion of the female wing of the police organization.

Saha (1989) conducted a study on Police Women "Femininity, a handicap?" The study suggested that in order to change the image, the serving women personnel have to display a matchless sense of duty, dedication and a spirit of selfless service. Only their performance can silence critics, challenge prejudices and frenzied campaigns and help them earn recognition and occupy a prestigious place in the police force, dominated by the stronger sex.

Aleem (1989) examined the role of women police in India, and is of the view that although women entered the Indian Police as early as 1938, their growth and development has been slow. By and large, women were used as social workers, rather than as law enforcement officers, dealing mainly with matters concerning women and children. For the past few decades, there has been an increase in the number of women joining the Indian police service. While some states are lagging behind, others have realized the importance of women in policing and thus there has been a drastic acceleration in the number of women joining the police force in these states.

Chakravarty (1994), in his article on "Equal opportunities to Women in Police" explains the results of discussions by a sample group of 39 male and female police officers of the rank of police Inspectors and Sub-Inspectors during the gender training organized at the Yashwantrao Chavan Academy of Development Administration, Pune, in November 1993. The theme developed and the rationale espoused in the note found positive response from the groups which were convinced that there was an urgent need to spread gender awareness in the police department and to change its prevailing gender biased policies, rules and practices. It was felt that there was an absolute necessity to open all walks of policing to women in order to bring women into the mainstream policing, instead of limiting them to the traditional 'Soft Sectors'.

Ghosh (1981) conducted a study on "Women in policing". It showed that attitudes towards employment of women police essentially have gone through a major change in the history of women police around the world. Women are seeking to prove that they can do the job of policing equally as well as the men.

Madhavan (2002) in her paper presented in Washington in "Women in Police" points out the complex issue of Law enforcement and Gender in India. She stresses on the fact that though the constitution of India guarantees gender justice, giving an equal opportunity for education, occupation to women, across the country in family and at workplace, women often continue to be victims of discrimination, harassment and crime. With concern to the above several issues are still relevant which need to be resolved. A core central issue is the concern for equal opportunity. The system has to ensure a level playing field if women are to have satisfaction and just advancement. Women leaders have to assert their role in ensuring this for the others. The need of the hour also is to motivate women in Police towards Continuous

Training and Development; Professionalism; Aim for Excellence and Stress on team playing.

Conclusion

Hence in the above chapter, an attempt has been made to review the existing studies concerning women police and various aspects of their role in society and family. Various problems faced by them in their work and at the place of work, perceptions and attitude of the public and victims towards women police and vice versa and their level of job satisfaction have been highlighted.

With regard to the variables considered above, opinion and views of various authors towards women police and their work has been portrayed, where by a lot of contradiction arises. For example, majority of the authors in their works have favoured the fact that women police equal men in their efficiency, skills and policing styles in almost all areas. This has been contradicted by other literature works whereby authors have stressed on the areas, where women policing still shows room for improvement. In a similar manner, a number of contradictory views are shown on the gender discrimination faced by women in their work place and the dual role of the women police both in their work and in the family.

The above studies also feature the fact that the women police were much more effective in handling violent situations. They are less likely to use excessive force and deal with victims in a much more sympathetic and communicative manner, compared to that of men.

Conclusively, the above chapter emphasises the need and significance of the study on evaluation of the performance of women police and the influencing factors, to be carried out, for which the methodology adopted has been presented in the forthcoming chapter.

3

Methodology

In this chapter, the methodology adopted for the present study is presented.

Statement of the Problem

The present research aims at studying the performance of the women police in the state of Tamil Nadu, the perception of the complainants / victims / witnesses / accused towards the women police and the problems faced by the women police while discharging their duties.

Objectives of the Study

1. To describe the history of the women police in India and in the State of Tamil Nadu.
2. To study the bio-demographic characteristics of the women police; reasons for choosing police work as a career; the attitude of the women police; difficulties faced by them within the family and outside; their working conditions; welfare measures provided to them by the department and the level of job satisfaction.

3. To study the bio-demographic characteristics of Victims/ Complainants; their reporting behaviour; the treatment of victims by the women police at the police station.

4. To study the bio-demographic characteristics of witnesses; the nature of the relationship between victims and witnesses; the treatment of witnesses by the women police at the police station.

5. To study the bio-demographic characteristics of the accused; their treatment at the time of arrest; and their treatment by the women police in the police station.

Variables Investigated

(i) Attitude of the women police towards policing.

(ii) Problems faced by the women police within the family and society.

(iii) Perception of the women police:

(iv) Working conditions of the women police.

(v) Welfare measures provided to the Police.

(vi) Level of job satisfaction.

(vii) Reporting behaviour of the victims/complainants with respect to their:

 (a) Age
 (b) Sex
 (c) Level of Education

(d) Occupation
(e) Level of income
(f) Religion
(g) Community
(h) Nativity

(viii) Treatment of the victims/complainants during investigation with respect to their:

(a) Age
(b) Sex
(c) Level of Education
(d) Occupation
(e) Level of income
(f) Religion
(g) Community
(h) Nativity

(ix) Treatment of witnesses at the police station with respect to their:

(a) Age
(b) Sex
(c) Level of Education
(d) Occupation
(e) Level of income
(f) Religion
(g) Community
(h) Nativity

(x) Treatment of the accused at the time of arrest by the women police with respect to their:

(a) Age
(b) Sex
(c) Level of Education
(d) Occupation
(e) Level of income
(f) Religion
(g) Community
(h) Nativity

(xi) Treatment of the accused at the police with respect to their:

(a) Age
(b) Sex
(c) Level of Education
(d) Occupation
(e) Level of income
(f) Religion
(g) Community
(h) Nativity

Research Design

Research designs broadly could be classified into two categories. (i) Basic research - which is primarily concerned for its quest for knowledge and knowing more about the phenomenon without concern for its practical use and also with developing and testing hypothesis and theories. This type of research is used to reject or support the existing theories about social phenomena (ii) Applied research: This research is concerned with search for ways of using scientific knowledge to solve practical problems. It is primarily focused on analyzing and solving social and real life problems. Research design can also be further classified into (i) Experimental research: which is conducted by controlling one or more variables and comparing control and experimental groups. (ii) Evaluation research: This research is usually conducted by sociologists, economists, psychologists and social workers to study the functioning of organizations to assess the existing policies and programmes of institutions to evaluate the utilization of funds received and so forth. Sarantakos (1998) has given the following goals of evaluation research: (i) to discover gaps in services, (ii) to investigate the alternative to meet the unmet needs, (iii) to predict whether a planned programme will be successful, (iv) to assess the effectiveness of the programme, (v) to establish whether the programme is cost- effective and whether benefits outweigh the cost, and (vi) to identify the ways of improving the effectiveness of the existing programme. The steps in evaluative research are the same as in other research which includes: Defining the problem, Sampling, Data Collection, Data Processing and Report Writing.

The research design of the present study is evaluation research. As one of the goals of evaluation research, in the cost benefit analysis both programme expenditure and the outcome are estimated in monetary terms and in the cost-effective analysis in which inputs are estimated in monetary terms while the outcome is estimated in terms of the actual impact. Sherman (1997) described the importance of the evaluation of efficiency in which he stated that "even though scientific evaluation results are a key part of rational policy analysis, those results cannot automatically select the best policy. This is due not just to the scientific limitation of generalizing results from one setting to the next but also due to the reason that evaluations often omit key data on cost benefit ratios. The fact that a programme is "effective" may be irrelevant to the financial or social costs being too high". The present research is an attempt to evaluate the performance of women police in general and the evaluation of their efficiency in particular. Therefore, this research falls under the category of evaluation research.

Hypotheses

The following hypotheses were formulated in the "null form" for the present research as no definite findings have been available from the previous researches in this specific field of study.

(i) The problems faced by women police in the family and society will not be associated with their bio-demographic, social and economic characteristics.

(ii) The problems faced by the women police in their family will not be related to their hours of duty.

(iii) Perception of working conditions of the women police will not differ significantly with reference to their bio-demographic, social and economic characteristics.

(iv) Perception of the women police about welfare measures provided by the police department will not differ significantly with reference to their bio-demographic, social and economic characteristics.

(v) Level of satisfaction of the women police will not differ significantly with reference to their bio-demographic, social and economic characteristics.

(vi) Average time taken to report the crime will not differ significantly with reference to their bio-demographic, social and economic characteristics.

(vii) Reasons for delay in reporting will not be associated with their bio-demographic, social and economic characteristics.

(viii) Treatment of victims/complainants at various stages of investigation will not be related to their bio-demographic, social and economic characteristics.

(ix) Treatment of witnesses at the police station will not be related to their bio demographic, social and economic characteristics.

(x) Treatment of accused at the time of arrest will not depend on their bio-demographic, social and economic characteristics.

(xi) Treatment of accused at the police station will not depend on their bio-demographic, social and economic characteristics.

Research Tool

(i) Construction of the Tool

In order to investigate the variables chosen for the study, the following interview schedules were constructed by the researcher:

1. An interview schedule for the Women Police in Tamil Nadu.
2. Methods of treatment of the victims/complainants by the women police.
3. Methods of treatment of witnesses by the women police.
4. Methods of treatment of accused by the women police.

Initially, the researcher generated a number of items comprehensively in order to measure each variable. The schedules were given to criminologists, criminal justice practitioners, psychometricians and statisticians. Then a pre-final version of each of the above tools were prepared.

In order to test the reliability and validity of the tool, a pilot study was conducted by administering the tools constructed to the subjects chosen for the study.

(ii) Description of the Tool

Interview Schedule I

The first interview schedule is—schedule about women police in the state of Tamil Nadu. This schedule has four parts and a job satisfaction inventory – which incorporates details with reference to the job security, working relationships with the superior and the promotion level of the women police.

Part I of the schedule contains 11 questions describing "a profile" of the women police such as their age, sex, educational qualifications, religion, community, marital status and nativity.

Part II of the schedule contains 9 questions pertaining to the reasons for choosing police work as a career, the reasons for quitting the previous job and the opinion of the women police about their present job. This section also incorporates items relating to the problems faced by the women police in their family and society and the extent of acceptance and recognition by the society.

Part III of the schedule contains 20 questions which relates to the working conditions of the women police, their hours of duty, the treatment they receive from their superiors in the department, various problems faced by them in their work and safety levels in their job, etc. It also includes items on the preferential treatment given to the women police, the time spent with their family and friends and in other recreation. Last but not the least, details with reference to the level of sexual harassment and discrimination faced by them in their places of duty has also been included in this part.

Part IV of the schedule contains 5 questions pertaining to the welfare measures provided to Women Police by the police department such as provision of residential quarters, provision of medical facilities, creche facilities and maternity leave.

Part V of the schedule contains items pertaining to the job satisfaction of the women police. It includes items such as the level of achievement and accomplishment in the job, the various conditions facilitating the job, the welfare measures and other opportunities provided for their advancement, the infrastructural facilities provided to them and the work load they have and also the opportunities for leadership and decision-making provided to them in their job.

Interview Schedule II

This deals with the methods of treatment of the victims/complainants by the women police. This interview schedule contains three parts.

Part I contains 11 items dealing with the personal details of the victims/complainants such as their age, sex, education, marital status, occupation, religion, community and nativity.

Part II of the schedule has items on the reception of victims/complainants at the police station as well as the reporting behaviour of the victims. It includes factors such as the duration of their wait at the police station, the time taken by them to report the crime to the police and the reasons for delay in reporting of the crime.

Part III of the schedule has 20 questions relating to the treatment given to the victims/complainants at the time of arrest, during the process of investigation and also during the trial of the case. It also includes items on their treatment at the police station like, if any care or sympathy was shown to them by the women police, if they were comforted and consoled, if prompt action was taken in their case and if they were counselled by the police. It also comprises items relating to various other processes during the investigation such as filing of the First Information Report (FIR), arrest of the accused, assistance rendered by the police to all the witnesses and the general opinion of the victims/ complainants about the performance of the women police in their case.

Interview Schedule III

This deals with the treatment of the witnesses at the police station by the women police. This schedule contains three parts.

Part I of the schedule has 11 items dealing with the personal details of the witnesses such as their age, sex, education, marital status, occupation, monthly income, religion, nativity and community.

Part II of the schedule has 3 questions relating to the nature of relationship of the witnesses with victims/ complainants/accused i.e. whether the witness is a friend or relative or neighbour or family member of the victims/complainants/accused.

Part III of the schedule comprises 12 questions pertaining to the treatment of the witnesses at the police station by the women police during the process of investigation of the case, i.e., whether they were treated with dignity, respect, politeness, kindness, sympathy and empathy. It also includes items on their reception at the police station i.e., whether they felt comfortable at the station, whether they were forced by the women police to depose evidence, whether the women police performed their duties fairly and lawfully, whether they were asked to give money or any other compliment to the police and finally their opinion on the performance of the women police in their case was also obtained.

Interview Schedule IV

This schedule is to evaluate the method of treatment of the accused by the women police. This schedule has three parts.

Part I of the schedule consists of 11 questions relating to the personal details of the accused such as their age, sex, education, marital status, occupation, monthly income, religion, community and nativity.

Part II of the schedule contains 7 questions on the treatment given to the accused, at the time of arrest by the women police. It also includes items on the nature of accusation, the place of arrest, whether they were called for counselling at the police station, whether they were informed of the reasons for their arrest, whether they were handcuffed at the time of arrest and whether they were produced before the appropriate courts within 24 hours of the arrest.

Part III of the schedule comprises 10 items to elicit information on the treatment given to the accused at the police station by the women police during interrogation such as informing them about their right to defence counsel, medical aid, free legal aid and provision of food during custody. It also includes questions such as information to their relatives about their arrest, whether the problem was settled through counselling, whether there was any attempt by the police officer to settle the issue which ended successfully, whether medical assistance was provided to them on request, whether they were permitted to meet their lawyer during interrogation and whether they were subjected to any kind of physical torture or verbal abuse.

(iii) Pilot Study

A pilot study was conducted with a sample size of 20 women police officers, 30 witnesses/victims/ accused. Before the pilot study, many items in the Interview Schedule were open ended and on the basis of the responses obtained, the Interview Schedule was structured. Therefore, in the final Interview Schedule only few items were kept as open ended and the remaining items in the Interview Schedule were structured and closed ended.

(iv) Reliability and Validity

With the help of the data collected through the pilot study, tests of reliability using the **split half co-efficient** method and validity were conducted for the tools and presented in Table 1.

Table 1.

Name of the Tool	*Reliability*	*Validity*
Women police in Tamil Nadu—An interview schedule.	0.8276*	0.8412*
Methods of treatment of the victims/complainants by women police.	0.7867*	0.8126*
Methods of treatment of witnesses by women police.	0.8210*	0.8620*
Methods of treatment of accused by women police	0.7992*	0.8315*

* $P < 0.01$

Universe of the Study

The universe of the present study comprises (a) women police in the State of Tamil Nadu particularly from the four districts, namely Chennai, Villupuram, Kancheepuram and Vellore; (b) the victims / complainants in the four districts namely Chennai, Villupuram, Kancheepuram and Vellore who had reported the crime in the respective All Women Police Stations in the year 1999; (c) the witnesses in the four districts, namely, Chennai, Villupuram, Kancheepuram and Vellore in the cases reported in the year 1999 in the All Women Police Stations of these districts; (d) the accused in the districts of Chennai, Villupuram, Kancheepuram and Vellore who were arrested for various offences dealt by the All Women Police Stations during the year 1999.

Sample and Sampling Procedure

A sampling design is a definite plan for obtaining a sample from a given population. It refers to the technique or the procedure the researcher would adopt in selecting items for the sample. It may as well lay down the number of items to be included in the sample, that is the size of the sample.

The sample in the present study comprises:

(a) Women police

(b) Victims/complainants

(c) Witnesses

(d) Accused

(a) In the case of the women police, a total number of 181 (as of July 2001) Women Police personnel are working in the four districts of Tamil Nadu namely Chennai, Villupuram, Kancheepuram and Vellore. The Researcher intended to include all the 181 women police personnel in the sample for the present study; but it so happened that 85 of the 181 were on leave or for various reasons were not available at the time of the study. Hence, the researcher was able to meet only 96 women police personnel who comprised the sample for the present study. These include police personnel of varying ranks ranging from Police Constables (Grade-I and Grade-II) to Sub-Inspectors and Inspectors of Police.

(b) The simple random sampling method was adopted to choose the sample of victims/complainants, witnesses and the accused from the list of victims/

complainants, witnesses and accused, obtained from the four police station jurisdictions in one year, that is, in 1999. In the case of victims/ complainants, out of a total population size of 2281, a sample size of 108 was chosen for the study using the simple random sampling procedure. Some of the victims identified by the simple random sampling method could not be interviewed because they had either shifted their place of residence or they had gone out for work. In a majority of the cases, the victim was found to be a female and they were mainly the victims of family disputes and domestic violence.

A similar procedure was adopted for the selection of witnesses and accused for the purpose of the study and a sample size of 75 witnesses and 60 accused was selected, from which only 71 witnesses and 57 accused were interviewed for the purpose of the study as, others were not available at the time of study for various reasons. The witnesses in most of the cases were the friends, neighbours or relatives of the victims/ complainants. As far as the accused were concerned, most of them were males and had been accused of various offences such as family disputes, domestic violence, harassment and dowry demand.

Statistical Analysis

The data collected were then processed by using statistical techniques such as **frequency analysis, correlation, chi-square and with non-parametric one way Analysis of Variance.**

(a) The purpose of **frequency analysis** is purely

descriptive and provides information on the distribution of a simple variable. This method was primarily employed to understand the bio-demographic details of the respondents and various other factors namely working conditions, welfare measures and treatment at the police station.

(b) **Correlation** gives information as to whether two variables are related or the changes in one variable relate to another. The investigator has also used Pearson Product Moment correlation to study the relationship between variables, when both the variables were continuous.

(c) The researcher has also utilised **Chi-square analysis** to determine the degree of association between the variables. It is a measure of the departure of obtained frequencies from the expected, by chance. The volume of chi-square ranges from zero [which indicates no departure, obtained from expected frequencies] to a large number of increasing values.

$$x^2 = \Sigma [(f_o - f_e)2/f_e]$$

(d) **Non parametric one way Analysis of Variance** - The Kruskal - Wallis test is analogous to one way analysis of variance. It can be used for experimental and non experimental data and is simple and effective. There may be cases in research, where it is possible to rank order the scores and then do the analysis on the ranks. There are also research situations in which the only form of measurement possible is rank order or ordinal measurement. The Kruskal - Wallis test is more useful in such situations.

$$H = \frac{12}{N(N+1)} S \frac{R^2}{n} - 3(N+1)$$

where

N = Total number of ranks

n = Number of ranks in one group

R = Sum of ranks in any one column

H is approximately distributed as ×2.

Degree of freedom K-1, where K is the numbers of columns or groups.

(e) The Mann-Whitney or Wilcoxon test is another non parametric test in which we combine the scores of both samples and scores of these from 1-19. We then focus on the score in the second sample. We count the number of scores in the first sample that have larger ranks and then add the results to give the statistics U.

$$\text{Mean} = \mu_U = \frac{N_1 \cdot N_2}{2}$$

$$\sigma_U = \sqrt{\frac{N_1 \cdot N_2 (N_1 + N_2 + 1)}{12}}$$

$$U = N_1 \cdot N_2 - U_1 \text{ or } U_1 = N_1 \cdot N_2 - U$$

If the number of cases is large or ties occur, it will probably be more convenient to obtain U by summing the ranks of separate samples calling these sum of ranks R1 and R2 and then using the formula

$$U = N_1.N_2 + \frac{N_2(N_2+1)}{2} - R_2$$

$$U_1 = N_1.N_2 + \frac{N_1(N_1+1)}{2} - R_1$$

$$Z = \frac{R_1 - R_2 - (N_1 - N_2)(N+1)/2}{N_1.N_2(N+1)/3}$$

Conclusion

From the above chapter, an easy understanding of the methodological approaches carried out for the present study of the performance of women police in Tamil Nadu has been facilitated. Inclusively, the objectives considered and the hypotheses adopted for the study have also been provided. By utilization of the variables considered for the study, an attempt has been made to obtain maximum data through interview schedules which covered details in various perspectives of the women police namely their performance, problems faced by them in their work, their relationship with society and family. The data obtained through the interview schedule were then subjected to statistical analysis by employing the above-described statistical tools, the results obtained for which have been discussed in the next chapter.

4

Results and Discussion

After the analysis of data, using appropriate statistical tools, the results obtained are presented in this chapter along with the discussion.

Characteristics and Performance of the Women Police in Tamil Nadu

Table 1. Profile of the Women Police

Sl. No		*Frequency*	*Percent*
1.	**Marital Status**		
	Married	85	88.6
	Spinster	10	10.4
	Widow	1	1.0
	Total	96	100.0
2.	**Nativity**		
	Rural	44	45.8
	Urban	52	54.2
	Total	96	100.0
3.	**Religion**		
	Hindu	87	90.6
	Muslim	2	2.1
	Christian	7	7.3
	Total	96	100.0
4.	**Community**		
	BC (Backward Class)	41	42.7
	MBC (Most Backward Class)	22	22.9
	SC (Scheduled Caste)	21	21.9
	ST (Scheduled Tribe)	1	1.0
	Others	11	11.5
	Total	96	100.0

(contd.)

Sl. No		*Frequency*	*Percent*
5.	**Educational Qualifications**		
	SSLC (Secondary School Leaving Certificate)	35	36.5
	PUC (PreUniversity Course)	31	32.3
	Graduate (B.A./B.Sc./B.Com.)	21	21.9
	Post Graduate (M.A./M.Sc./M.Com.)	8	8.3
	Others	1	1.0
	Total	96	100.0

As far as the marital status is concerned, it is evident from the above table that a majority (88.6%) of the respondents are married, 10.4% of them are spinsters and 1% of them are widows. Of the total number of respondents, 45.8% hail from rural areas and the remaining 54.2% of the respondents hail from urban areas.

It is also evident that a majority (90.6%) of the respondents are Hindus. A small percentage (2.1%) of the sample are Muslims and 7.3% are Christians. Muslim families are generally orthodox and conservative. The parents and husbands do not generally prefer their women folk taking up a job. Even if they decide to take up some employment, joining the police department is not preferred. Also, the literacy rate among Muslim women is comparatively less and that accounts for the less percentage of Muslim women in the police department.

With regard to the community background of the women police, it is evident from Table 1 that 42.7% of the sample belong to the Backward Class; 22.9% fall under the Most Backward Class; 21.9% belong to the Scheduled Caste; and a negligible 1 per cent belong to the Scheduled Tribe. The remaining 11.5% of the sample belong to other communities. As per the current policy on communal rotation, the recruitment of women in the police has exceeded the prescribed quota and this may be attributed to increased education and employment opportunities in the police department. The craze for uniforms and influence of the parents and relatives with police background could have made an impact on the mind of the women in joining the police department. Illiteracy, economic backwardness and other social factors such as early marriage, lack of minimum physical requirements etc. may be some of the reasons for lesser percentage in the recruitment of women in the police department from the scheduled tribe community.

As far as the educational background of the respondents is concerned, it was found that a majority of the respondents have acquired only the School/Pre-University Education (SSLC - 36.5%; PUC - 32.3%). It is also found that 21.9% of the sample are graduates and 8.3% of the sample have obtained postgraduate degrees. The minimum qualification required for joining the police force is a pass in High School. Women discontinue their education at the High School final level due to the pressure of financial burden of their families. The opening in the police force for women with a minimum qualification of a pass in High School is a welcome opportunity for them. Thus women opt for this job to support their families economically.

The above table reflects the general family background of the respondents.

Table 2. Family background of the respondents and their opinion about their job

Sl. No			Frequency	Percent
1.	**Occupation of Father**			
	Unemployed		24	25.0
	Farmer		26	27.1
	Business		7	7.3
	Office		10	10.4
	Police		14	14.6
	Professional		2	2.1
	Retired		13	13.5
		Total	96	100.0
2.	**Occupation of Husband**			
	Unemployed		13	13.6
	Farmer		3	3.1
	Business		10	10.4
	Office		43	44.8
	Police		20	20.8
	Professional		4	4.2
	Retired		3	3.1
		Total	96	100.0
3.	Is your husband co-operative?	No comment	6	6.3
		Yes	77	80.2
		No	13	13.5
		Total	96	100.0
4.	How do your husband/ parents feel about your working with men?	Accept	3	3.1
		Unhappy	75	78.1
		Do not mind	7	7.3
		Suspicious	8	8.3
		No response	3	3.1
		Total	96	100.0
5.	How do your mother-in-law, father-in-law and other in-laws consider your job?	Happy	10	10.4
		Unhappy	60	62.5
		Indifferent	16	16.7
		No response	10	10.4
		Total	96	100.0

When discussing the occupation of the father of the respondents, it was found that in 25% of the cases, the fathers of the women police were unemployed; 27.1% of them were farmers, 7.3% of them were into business; 10.4% office-goers; 14.6% employed in the police department; 13.5% retired and a meagre 2.1% of them were professionals.

As far as the occupation of the husband is concerned, in 44.8% of the cases, the husbands of the women police were office-goers. In 20.8% of the cases, their husbands worked in the same department, i.e. Police department; 10.4% were into business; 13.6% were unemployed; 4.2% professionals; 3.1% farmers and an equal percentage of them were retired.

An attempt was also made to analyze the reaction of the family members of the respondents towards their present job. They were asked, if their husbands were co-operative and helped them in their work and other areas. It was found that in most of the cases, the respondents' husbands (80.2%) were co-operative and helpful to them, while a few of them (13.5%) were not so. Quite a few of them (6.3%) chose not to answer this question. It was further found that the husbands of the women police were co-operative mostly in those cases where they themselves were in the police services or where the marriage was of an endogamous type. In cases where the husbands were civilians, they rendered not much help to their wives because they could not relate to the working patterns of their wives and their working with male colleagues. Also, there were ego clashes between the husbands and wives, if they were working in different areas. When asked about the behaviour of their parents/husbands, towards their job and their nature of work, in 78.1% of the cases, the respondents opined that their parents/husband were unhappy about their working with other men. In 3.1% of the cases, the husband/parents accepted their working with men, while in 7.3% of the cases, the family members did not actually mind their working with men. In 8.3% of the cases, the husbands/parents were suspicious about their wife/daughter working with men.

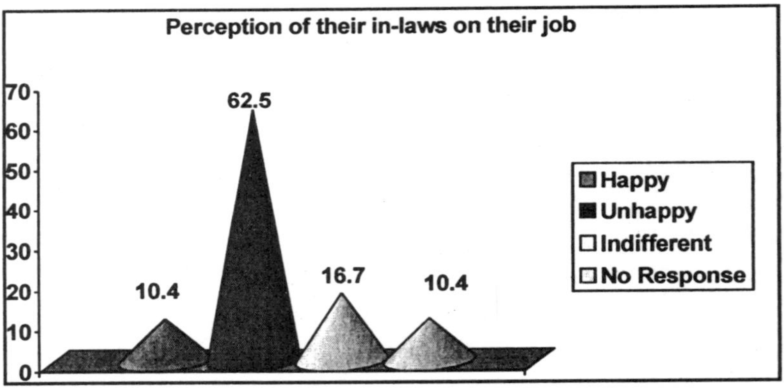

Fig. 1.

When asked about the reaction of their in-laws towards their present job, it was observed that a fair number of respondents (62.5%) opined that their in-laws were not happy about their jobs. A small percentage of them (10.4%) said that their in-laws were happy with their job. About 16.7% of them said that their in-laws were indifferent towards their present job. Towards any woman outstandingly visible, the first reaction of the society is one of repulsion and submission. The attitude is "After all —'a woman'." A woman can easily be drawn into scandals and willing rumours. The best weapon that comes handy to the gender stretching community will be a psychological and moral assault. Women in police become easy victims to character assassination intended to show them their place. The unhappiness of a large majority of the in-laws may be attributed to their conservative and narrow-minded attitude. Most of the in-laws do not like their daughters-in-law mingling with other men folk while working. Since the women police have to be on duty round the clock, they get very little time to spend with their family, children etc. Also, the nature of job of the women police demands, sometimes, working late in the night or even going for night shifts and this definitely is not an acceptable trend in the conservative family environment that prevails. This results in dissatisfaction of in-laws with their daughters-in-law. Some of the in-laws feel that their daughters-in-law is not meant for such a job and so they are unhappy with her job. There are, however, in-laws who recognize and appreciate the capabilities and potential of their daughters-in-law and have respect for her profession. As inferred from the table, a vast majority of the family members of the women police are not particularly happy about their working with other men in their job in office. A prime reason for this unhappiness can be attributed to the conservative nature of the family members and the social norms, deviating from which, means a sin.

Table 3. Availability of Time for Family and Recreation.

		Every Day		Once in Few Days		Once in A Week		Once in a Month		Once in Few Months	
		Frequency	Percent	Frequency	Percent	Frequency	Percent	Frequency	Percent	Frequency	Percent
(a)	With their family	15	15.6	11	11.4	21	21.8	38	39.5	11	11.7
(b)	Sports and Games	1	1.1	3	3.2	-	-	7	7.2	85	88.5
(c)	Reading	5	5.2	11	11.4	16	16.6	13	13.6	51	53.2
(d)	Entertainment	-	-	2	3	1	1	24	25.0	69	71
(e)	Other Hobbies	-	-	1	1	1	1	11	11.4	83	86.6
(f)	Leisure Activities	1	1	-	-	-	-	1	1	94	98

It is clear from the above table that the women police are so engaged in their work that they do not have sufficient time to spend with their families. They are so tied up, that there is hardly any time for any recreational activities such as sports, games and reading. Such a busy schedule would indeed make their work very monotonous and this would have a direct impact on their efficiency and performance. It would also be difficult to expect job satisfaction from them amidst such a busy work schedule with almost no time for family and friends or any other kind of recreation or entertainment.

The respondents were asked for reasons as to why they chose police service in particular as their career. There were different reasons given by them for choosing this as their profession. In 20.8% of the cases, the respondents joined the police service, as they were not

Table 4. Job details

1.	*Reasons for choosing Police work as a career.*	*Frequency*	*Percent*
(i)	Did not get any other job	20	20.8
(ii)	Interested in police work since childhood days	29	30.2
(iii)	Can help people in many ways	31	32.3
(iv)	Parents/Husband forced to join the police force	6	6.3
(v)	Job Security	7	7.3
(vi)	Other reasons	3	3.1
	Total	96	100.0
2.	**Whether the present job is the first employment?**		
(i)	Yes	86	89.6
(ii)	No	10	10.4
	Total	96	100.0
3.	**Reasons for quitting the previous job.**		
(i)	More monetary benefit in the present job	80	83.3
(ii)	More fringe benefits in the present job	3	3.1
(iii)	More power and prestige in the present job	3	3.1
(iv)	More respect from the public in the present job	6	6.3
(v)	To render service to the public	2	2.1
(vi)	Other reasons	2	2.1
	Total	96	100.0

able to get any other job. Similarly, 7.3% of the respondents joined the force for job security. Another 6.3% of them said that their parents/husbands forced them to join the police force. Having a police background or acquaintances of police background had instilled a passion for this job in some of them. It is interesting to note that in 30.2% of the cases, the respondents said that they joined the police force, as they were interested in police work since their

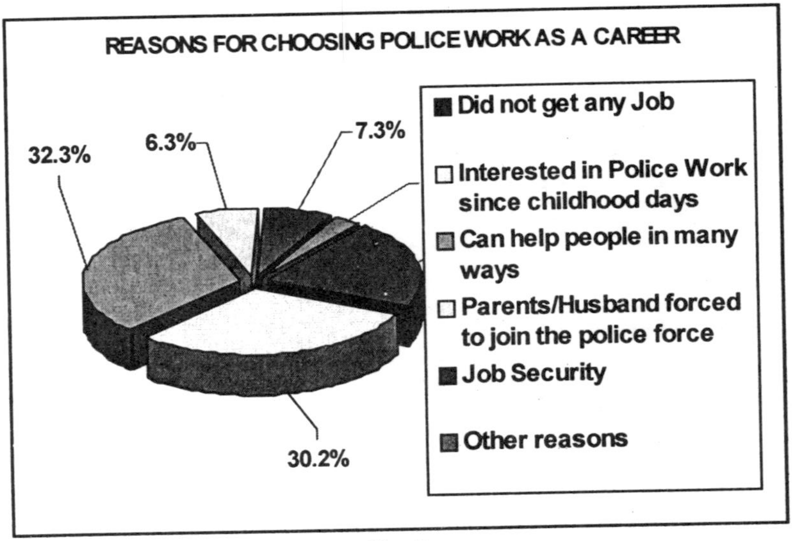

Fig. 2.

childhood. The powers the police possess, which they did not as civilians, enable them to serve many causes in a progressive and rightful way. 32.3% of the respondents said that the police force as they beheld was a powerful means to serve people in many ways.

Questions pertaining to their employment were also put forward to the respondents. They were asked if the present police work was their first employment or whether they had been working with some other organization previously. The response given by the respondents is presented in the given table. In 89.6% of the cases, the respondents opined that the present job in the police force was their first employment. For the remaining 10.4% of the respondents, it was not the first employment as they had already worked elsewhere before taking up the present employment.

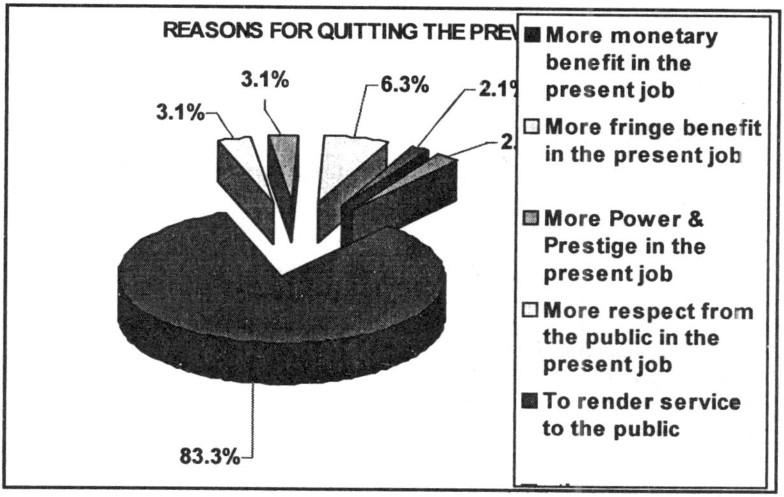

Fig. 3.

The respondents were also asked the reasons for quitting their previous job and choosing the present employment. There were different reasons cited by them for this question. A vast majority (83.3%) of the sample had quit the job as they found more monetary benefits in their present job. 3.1% of the sample found more fringe benefits in the present job. Another 3.1% of the sample quit the previous job and opted for the present one, for the power and prestige that they observed in the present job. Another 6.3% of the sample felt that there was more respect from the public if they joined the women police. Another 2.1% of the population quit the previous job and took up the present one, as they wanted to render the service to the public.

When assessing the mode of appointment of the respondents, it was found that a very small percentage

(2.1%) of the women police were appointed for their excellence in sports. Appointment based on compassionate grounds is very less (3.1%) and appointment through other means has also been very less (1%) while direct appointment to the service stands out (93.8%).

Table 5. Job Satisfaction

		Frequency	*Percent*
Do you feel that your job in the police department is better than the jobs in other departments?	Yes	48	50.0
	No	48	50.0
	Total	96	100.0
Do you feel that the police job suits your ability?	Yes	92	95.8
	No	4	4.2
	Total	96	100.0
Would you like to continue this job till your retirement?	Yes	78	81.2
	No	18	18.8
	Total	96	100.0
Do your family and friends recognize and appreciate you in this job?	Yes	71	74.0
	No	25	26.0
	Total	96	100.0
Do you feel that the society recognizes your job as a woman police?	Yes	87	90.6
	No	9	9.4
	Total	96	100.0
Do you feel that the Women Police have gained the confidence of the society?	Yes	87	90.6
	No	9	9.4
	Total	96	100.0

50% of the sample expressed that their job in the Police Department was better than the jobs in the other departments (PWD/Revenue, Social Welfare Organization and Private Organizations). Remaining

50% of them expressed negatively that there is no rest hour for them at the workplace. It involves a lot of physical and mental strain. They have no fixed work hours.

They were also asked if, in their opinion the present job matched with their abilities and whether they felt that they were performing to the best of their abilities in their job. In a large majority of the cases (95.8%), the respondents felt that the police job suited their ability whereas the remaining 4.2% of the respondents were of the opinion that their present job did not suit their ability. The positive response from a large majority of the sample also indicated that they wanted to continue their present job for a long time and had no plans of quitting the job. This was seen in 81.3% of the cases. It was only in 18.8% of the cases where the respondents felt the other way. Apart from the job satisfaction, another reason for which the respondents wanted to stick to their present job for a longer period was that in 74% of the cases, the respondents felt that they got their due respect and recognition and appreciation from the general society, family and friends. Hence, they were happy and well satisfied with their present job. It was only in 26% of the cases that the respondents felt that they did not really get the respect and appreciation from their family and friends.

They were also enquired whether they earned the due respect and recognition from the society in general. It was observed that in 90.6% of the cases, the respondents were of the opinion that the society recognized their job as women police, where as in the remaining 9.4% of the cases, there was a lack of such recognition in the society. Women police are found to be more compassionate and sympathetic than their male counterparts. Also, they are equally efficient at work and are able to help the children, women in distress and the aged and hence have earned due recognition in the society for their services. Although in a majority of the cases, the respondents opined that they get the recognition of the society for their service and performance, in some cases they find difficulty in getting whole hearted co-operation from their family members.

They were also asked if they felt, they were successful in gaining the confidence of the society. There was a positive response from a large number of the sample (90.6%) revealing that the Women Police have not only gained the confidence of the society but also handled their job efficiently. Only in 9.4% of the cases, the respondents gave a negative response. As far as gaining the confidence of the society is concerned, particular emphasis can be laid on gaining the confidence of the womenfolk in the society. The All Women Police Stations were established keeping in mind the welfare and convenience of other womenfolk in the society, who are suffering and are not in a position to present their problems to the male police officers effectively due to various personal and social reasons. Moreover, the male police officers have been criticized for being suspicious of the motives of women who make complaints of sexual assault, for dismissing appeals for help, for reluctance to pursue investigations and press charges. Criticism has also been focused on poor facilities available and procedures for dealing with victims and gathering evidence. According to the respondents, a large majority of women are coming forward to these police stations to seek remedy to all their problems, be it personal or otherwise. These increasing percentages of complainants signify the trust and confidence gained by the women police. It also reveals that they are capable of handling their job efficiently.

Table 6. Working Conditions

S.No		Yes	No
1.	Are you satisfied with the working patterns (7 days a week, patrolling duty, escorting criminals and checking of women passengers)	66 (68.8)	30 (31.3)
2.	Are you satisfied with the working hours (24 hours duty)	29 (30.2)	67 (69.8)
3.	Number of working hours 7-8 hours 9-10 hours 11 hours and more	 55 4 37	 57.3 4.2 38.5
	Total	96	100.0
4.	Are you able to avail off duty on certain occasions and festivals?	56 (58.3)	40 (41.7)
5.	Is the duration of maternity leave provided for the common police engaged in the out door work adequate?	40 (41.7)	56 (58.3)
6.	Do you have any get-together functions, cultural festivals, especially organized for you by your department?	7 (7.3)	89 (92.7)

It is equally important to know that the working conditions of the women police also play a major role in achieving job satisfaction and performing to the best of their abilities.

When asked if they were satisfied with their working pattern, it was found that in 68.8% of the cases, the respondents were satisfied with their working pattern where as the remaining 31.2% expressed dissatisfaction. The women police are not regarded to have functional capacities equal to their male peers. Hence, they are mostly given light responsibilities that require relatively soft handling and one visible extension of their traditional role as women. They are allotted jobs like patrolling, checking of women passengers, regulating festival crowds and cinema crowds. However, none of these jobs are part of the mainstream policing. Hence, this contributes to the dissatisfaction in a small percentage of the women police. In addition, the women police do not really like checking the passengers. They also do not prefer regulating crowds during festivals as they face a lot of ill treatment by agitators and processionists.

In addition, the dissatisfaction expressed by 69.8% of the respondents concerning the working hours has outnumbered the ones satisfied (30.2%) with the working hours. As seen from the table, majority of the respondents are not comfortable with the working hours. Their schedule is tedious. They are given 24 hours duty and they have regular night shifts. Even if they are given a day off, they are called back in case of any emergency. Consequently, they do not have much time to devote towards their family and children. They are also unable to fulfill their personal responsibilities. Most of the respondents felt that a regular shift system would be convenient.

They were first asked about their working hours and work pattern. It was found that a considerable percentage (38.5%) of the respondents said that they work for more than 11 hours a day. However, a majority (57.3%) of the respondents said that they have to work for about 7-8 hours a day. 4.2% of the respondents said that they have to work for about 9-11 hours a day. The women police are normally engaged in duties like patrolling, bandobust duties, escorting criminals and regulating crowd, which consume most of their time and energy and thus demands extra work hours per day.

From the above Table (Table No. 3), it is evident that 58.3% of the sample opined that they were able to avail 'off duty' on certain/compelling occasions and festivals whereas 41.7% of them said that they were not able to do so. The women police are allotted different kinds of duties such as patrolling, bandobust, escorting prisoners etc. and their presence is very important at the allotted place of duty. They are normally given 'leave' on certain/compelling occasions and festivals. But if there is any emergency where their presence is felt necessary, their leave may be cancelled and they may be called back to work. In certain other cases, they may not be granted leave at all. Also, due to the nature of work the women police have to perform, they are expected to come even on general holidays. Therefore, some of them may not be able to avail off duty on certain/compelling occasions and festivals.

Also, it can be inferred from the above table that in 41.7% of the cases, the respondents were of the opinion that the duration of maternity leave provided to them was adequate whereas the remaining 58.3% of the respondents felt that the leave provided to them was inadequate. The maternity leave that is provided to the women police covers only the period until the delivery of the child. It does not take into account the post-delivery period. The women police who are normally engaged in outdoor work need a lot of rest before they get back to work. Hence, most of them opined that the actual leave granted to them was inadequate. Also, in certain families, there may not be anyone to look after the child and the child may be too young to be left either in a crèche or under the care of a governess. So, most of the police women felt that the maternity leave provided to them by the department was inadequate.

Questions pertaining to the level of safety in the job were also put forth to the respondents and the feeling of the respondents with reference to the same was noted. It was observed that 86.5% of the respondents felt safe in their job. 13.5% of the respondents involved had a negative reply because of the insecurities, assaults and physical harassment. It has been found that in most of the cases where the women police had to confront a critical situation, the men police had to back them up and escort them when needed. Therefore, they always tend to have a support system when facing dangerous situations. As far as matters of family disputes are concerned, the women police handle the situation on their own. The women police felt insecure about returning home all alone at odd hours in the night and also when going out for an enquiry of any case all alone. Otherwise, most of the women police were found to be satisfied with the safety level in their job.

Table 7. Safety Levels of the Job

S.No	*Safety levels of job*	*Yes*	*No*
1.	Do you feel the safety level in your job is satisfactory? [safety level — safety from criminals, assaults, physical safety].	83 (86.5)	13 (13.5)
2.	Do you feel that the processionists or agitators ill-treat or tease you while you are engaged in crowd regulation?	48 (50.0)	48 (50.0)
3.	Do you feel that the female processionists or agitators ill-treat or tease you while you are engaged in regulations?	31 (32.3)	65 (67.7)
4.	Are you satisfied with the present design of uniform?	92 (95.8)	4 (4.2)
5.	Is the present uniform convenient and safe to discharge your duties?	95 (99.0)	1 (1.0)
6.	Are you satisfied with the weapons provided by the department?	82 (85.4)	14 (14.6)

When asked about the behaviour of the public towards them while engaging in crowd regulation, it was observed that in 50% of the cases, respondents affirmed that they were ill-treated or teased by processionists or agitators when engaged in crowd regulation. The other 50% of the respondents denied the same. The probable reason for the ill-treatment of the women police by processionists or agitators may be that, women are still considered to be the weaker sex in the society and a woman police is regarded as a woman first and then as a police officer. That is why some of them are either ill-treated or teased by processionists and agitators. when engaged in crowd regulation despite their being in uniform. When asked about the ill-treatment by female processionists/ agitators, 67.7% of the respondents opined that they were neither ill-treated nor teased by female processionists or agitators while they were engaged in crowd regulations, but a considerable number (32.3%) contradictorily said that they were ill-treated or teased by female processionists or agitators.

As far as their uniform was concerned, it was observed that in 95.8% of the cases, the respondents were satisfied with the present design of uniform while 4.2% of the respondents expressed their dissatisfaction with the same. As seen from the table, a vast majority of the respondents expressed satisfaction with their present uniform design. One of the reasons for this was that the present uniform was comfortable to wear when compared to the traditional Indian costumes like a saree or salwar. Also, the uniform in itself commanded respect from people in the society. It also boosted their self-confidence and morale. In addition, a majority (99%) of the respondents felt that the present uniform was convenient as well as safe for them while discharging their duties.

The respondents were further asked if they were happy with the kind of weapons provided to them by the department as they also play a major role in their safety in physically unsafe situations. In 85.4% of the cases, the respondents were found to be satisfied with the weapons that were provided to them by their department. In 14.6% of the cases, the respondents expressed dissatisfaction with the same. This dissatisfaction of a small percentage of the respondents was with the provision of depositing or safeguarding the weapons that are provided to them. They were of the opinion that there was no proper provision of safeguarding their weapons and on most of the occasions, they were forced to deposit their weapons in the men police stations. Also, the women police stations were not provided with wireless sets. Other necessary provisions like raincoats, gumboots, or walkie-talkies were also not provided. Rifles were provided to them only recently. This added to the dissatisfaction of a small percentage of the women police.

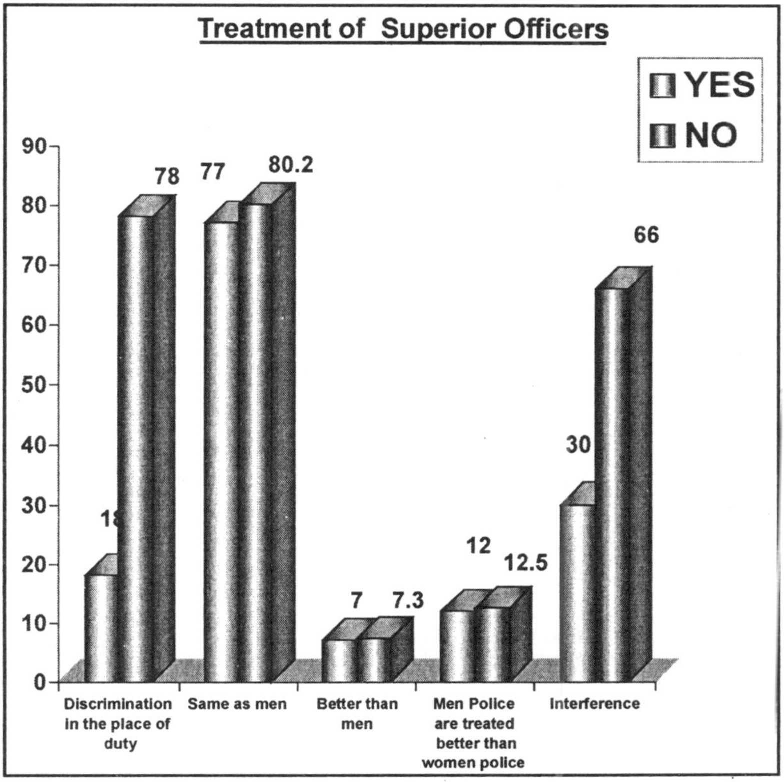

Fig. 4.

The above table explains the treatment meted out to the respondents by their department superiors and other colleagues.

As far as discrimination at the work place based on sex is concerned, it is evident that 81.2% of the respondents felt that there was no discrimination at the place of duty on the basis of sex. It was found that the

Table 8. Treatment of Superior Officers

S.No		Yes	No
1.	Do you feel that there is discrimination in the place of duty on the basis of sex?	18 (18.8)	78 (81.2)
2.	Preferential treatment given to women police:		
	While assigning tasks	24 (25)	72 (75)
	In job placements	18 (18.8)	78 (81.2)
3.	What type of treatment do you get from your superiors in the Department, when compared to Men Police?		
	Same as men. Better than men. Men Police are treated better than women Police.	77 7 12	80.2 7.3 12.5
	Total	96	100.0
		Yes	**No**
4.	Opinion of the respondents with respect to preferential treatment and efficiency at work?		
	Increase the efficiency at work. Decrease the efficiency at work No difference	39 3 54	40.6 3.1 56.3
	Total	96	100.0
5.	Is your job free from interference of your department superiors?	30 (31.2)	66 (68.8)
6.	Do you get any help & assistance from your supervisors in discharging your duties?	7 (7.3)	89 (92.7)
7.	Do you feel that there is sexual harassment in the place of duty?	18 (18.8)	78 (81.2)

18.8% of the respondents said that there was discrimination on the basis of sex in the place of work. They are still viewed as 'women' first and as police personnel next. Their gender is first taken into consideration before they are assigned any duty and there is a bias in assigning them their tasks. Therefore, the respondents generally feel that there is discrimination in the place of duty on the basis of sex. Wyles (1952) conducted a similar study on "Women at Scotland Yard". It shows that generally the women police officers in sharp contrast to their male colleagues believe that they are discriminated against. The policemen are prejudiced against them. Further, they greatly overemphasize the importance of physical strength in the job that women are effectively excluded from some of the more interesting kinds of work and that men do not accept them as full members of the working group or as colleagues on an equal basis.

The respondents were also asked if any preferential treatment was given to them because of being a woman in the police department. 25% of the respondents said that they were given preferential treatment while assigning tasks; 18.8% of them said that they were given preferential treatment in job placement; but a majority (75%) of the respondents opined that they were not given any kind of preferential treatment either while assigning them tasks or in job placement. Although women entered the police services as early as 1938, they have not been fully accepted by their male colleagues. Their male colleagues or superiors do not still consider them as 'equals'. Even today, they are viewed as 'females' first and also as being 'soft and delicate' and consequently, some of the officers, in certain situations show a preferential attitude towards them while assigning them tasks to do or while placing them in jobs. A majority of the respondents (80.2%) further opined that they were treated in the same manner as men police by their superiors in the department. A few (7.3%) of the respondents said that the treatment they got from their superiors was better than the one they got from their male counterparts. The remaining 12.5% of the respondents opined that the men police were treated better than them by their superiors. It is heartening to note that in majority of the cases, the women police are of the opinion that their superior officers in the department treated them on par with men. In certain cases, they were treated even better than the men. This goes a long way to explain that the era of acceptance of women police in services has begun and that their colleagues and superiors are recognizing them. In certain cases, men police are treated better than women police and this preferential treatment may be attributed to the nature of work they are assigned. The women police get better treatment than the men police in cases where they are at higher level posts, extracting duties from others.

With regard to the opinion of the respondents towards preferential treatment given to them and efficiency at work, the table shows that 40.6% of the sample opined that preferential treatment would increase the efficiency at work where as only 3.1% expressed that preferential treatment would decrease the efficiency at work. A majority of the respondents

(56.3%) felt that there is no difference in their efficiency at work due to preferential treatment given to them.

In a majority of the cases, the respondents opined that preferential treatment had nothing to do with the efficiency at work. Their efficiency depended solely upon their hard work and sincerity and not on any kind of preferential treatment shown to them. There were, however policewomen who felt that they could perform better if they were given preference and importance by their superiors and colleagues. Surprisingly in a few cases, the preferential treatment had decreased the efficiency of the women police at work.

An attempt was also made to analyze the extent to which the women police worked independently without any interference in their work. It was found that in 68.8% of the cases, their job was not free from interference of their department superiors, politicians and other influential persons but quite a few (31.2%) said that their job was free from any kind of interference by their department superiors, politicians and other influential persons. Women, who enter gender inappropriate occupations and numerically skewed groups, experience negative consequences such as performance pressures, social isolation and role encapsulation. Being few in number, the women police receive heightened attention or visibility that exacerbate pressures for them to perform well. Apart from this, they are pressurized from all sides including their department superiors, politicians, lawyers and other influential persons preventing them from taking any action against the accused in case the accused is well known to them. The department superiors tend to exhibit a dominant behaviour in case they insist on taking appropriate action in the case. Also, since the women police wing has been started only recently, the supervisory officers often tend to guide the women police in various respects and this is often resented by them and is viewed as an interference of department superiors in their regular work.

Also, when they were asked about the help and assistance rendered by their superiors, it was found that only a small percentage (7.3%) were able to get help and assistance from their superiors in discharging their duties where as in 92.7% of the cases, the respondents denied getting any help or assistance from their superiors. It is regrettable to note that in majority of the cases, the women police did not get any help or assistance from their superiors while discharging their duties. The probable reason for non-co-operation from their department superiors could be due to the misunderstandings between them or it may be due to ego clashes. In addition, if the superior officer is on leave or if the post of the officer is vacant, in those cases also there would be no assistance rendered to them by the superior officers in discharging their duties.

When asked about the sexual harassment (if any) at the work place, 81.2% of the respondents expressed that there was no sexual harassment at the place of duty where as 18.8% felt that there was sexual harassment at the place of duty. The admitting of 18% sexual harassment in the workplace is a matter of serious concern since the women police themselves have to enforce laws against the harassment of women in working places. The harassment of women police at the workplace is normally by their superiors, colleagues, or subordinates. At times, they are even harassed by the public. The attitude that a woman, no matter what her profession or position is, is still a woman, is the root cause of such harassment.

Table 9. Facilities Provided

S.No		Yes	No
1.	Are you satisfied with the facilities exclusively required for women, which have been provided by the department?	24 (25.0)	72 (75.0)
2.	Have you been provided with residential quarters for your family?	48 (50.0)	48 (50.0)
3.	Do you feel that a crèche facility should be made available near your work place?	66 (68.8)	30 (31.2)
4.	Do you feel that the welfare measures regarding medical-aid and general health provided by your department are adequate?	17 (17.7)	79 (82.3)

The respondents were asked about the facilities that were provided to them by their department. This included various aspects such as medical facilities, creche facilities and other necessary assistance provided at work. Questions were asked pertaining to the facilities provided by the department to them at their place of work. It was found that most of the respondents (75%) were not satisfied with the facilities provided by the department that were exclusively required for women and only 25% of the respondents were satisfied with the facilities provided to them. A vast majority of the respondents opined that there was a lack of facilities that must actually be provided to them by their department. There were no proper sanitation facilities. The buildings did not have proper toilets. Their problems were never attended to. At times, they even had no place to sit in their own office. The vehicle that was provided to them was often used by other male police officers and therefore, they had no vehicle in case of any emergency.

With regard to the facilities (such as residential quarters) provided by the department, it was found that 50% of the respondents stated that their families were provided with residential quarters and the other half were not provided with the same. As evident from the table, in 50% of the cases, the women police have not been provided with residential quarters. This is mainly because the ratio of housing accommodation with respect to strength of the women police is only 40-50%. Therefore, it is difficult to provide all of them with residential quarters. They are of the opinion that there are various aspects like distance, high rent and transportation that are of concern for them. Their place of stay outside has lot of such discomforting factors including returning home late after duty. So, they feel that it would be better if they were provided with quarters to stay. This would enhance their level of job satisfaction.

As far as the welfare measures such as medical aid etc. was concerned, it was found that though 17.7% of the respondents felt that the welfare measures regarding medical-aid and general health provided by their department was adequate, yet 82.3% of them felt that such welfare measures were inadequate. As seen from the table, a vast majority of the respondents were not really satisfied with the medical-aid and general health facility provided by the department. Though the department has made compulsory provisions relating to the biennial medical examination of all the police personnel, there are however, no provisions to deal with the immediate problems that the women police might face. The health complication like abortion during pregnancy is not immediately attended because of the lack of medical attention in their workplaces, which lead to the dejection among women police. This adds to the dissatisfaction of a vast majority of the women police.

Methods of Treatment of the Victims/Complainants by Women Police in Tamil Nadu

Table 10. Profile of Victims/Complainants

Sl. No.		*Frequency*	*Percent*
1.	**Age**		
	Upto 25 years	45	41.7
	25-50 years	60	55.6
	Above 50 years	3	2.7
	Total	108	100.0
2.	**Sex**		
	Male	6	5.6
	Female	102	94.4
	Total	108	100.0
3.	**Marital Status**		
	Married	64	59.2
	Unmarried	7	6.5
	Divorced	3	2.8
	Widow	1	0.9
	Separated	33	30.6
	Total	108	100.0

(contd.)

Sl. No.		Frequency	Percent
4.	**Religion**		
	Hindu	85	78.7
	Muslim	13	12.0
	Christian	10	9.3
	Total	108	100.0
5.	**Nativity**		
	Rural	54	50.0
	Urban	54	50.0
	Total	108	100.0

The above table explains the bio-demographic characteristics of the victims/complainants.

The above table shows that 41.7% of the respondents are within 25 years of age, 55.6% of the respondents are between 25-50 years of age and 2.7% of the respondents are above 50 years. It can be inferred from the above table that majority of the victims/complainants fall in the age group between 25-50 years.

As far as the gender is concerned 94.4% of the respondents were females and only 5.6% of the respondents were males.

Of the total number of respondents chosen for the study, 59.2% of the respondents were married; 30.6% were separated; 6.5% were unmarried; 2.8% of the respondents were divorced and a meagre 0.9% of the respondents were widows.

Also, a vast majority (78.7%) of the respondents belonged to Hinduism; 12% of them were Muslims and the remaining 9.3% were Christians. Half of the population hailed from the rural areas and the remaining half of the population hailed from the urban.

Table 11. Profile of Victims/Complainant

Sl. No.		*Frequency*	*Percent*
1.	**Education**		
	Illiterate	32	29.6
	Upto 5th Standard	22	20.4
	Upto 10th Standard	34	31.5
	Upto 12th Standard	4	3.7
	Under Graduate	12	11.1
	Post Graduate	4	3.7
	Total	108	100.0
2.	**Occupation**		
	No job	16	14.8
	Housemaid	54	50.0
	Daily wage earner	31	28.7
	Office	3	2.8
	Business	3	2.8
	Professional	1	0.9
	Total	108	100.0
3.	**Nature of Family**		
	Joint	34	31.5
	Nuclear	74	68.5
	Total	108	100.0
4.	**Monthly Income**		
	Upto Rs. 500	34	31.5
	Rs. 501- Rs. 1500	46	42.6
	Rs. 1501- Rs. 2500	13	12.1
	Rs. 2501- Rs. 3500	5	4.6
	Above Rs. 3500	10	9.2
	Total	108	100.0

With regard to educational qualifications of the respondents, the table explains that 29.6% of the respondents were illiterates; 20.4% had obtained education upto 5th standard, 31.5% had obtained education upto 10th standard, 3.7% had studied till 12th; 11.1% had obtained their graduation degrees and a meagre 3.7% of the respondents had completed their post graduation.

The occupational pattern of the respondents indicate that a majority (50%) of them were housemaids; 28.7% of the respondents worked on the basis of daily wages; 14.8% of the respondents were unemployed; an equal percentage (2.8%) of the respondents were office goers or in business and a meagre 0.9% of the respondents were professionals.

As far as the family pattern was concerned, 68.5% of the respondents were a nuclear family whereas the remaining 31.5% of them lived in joint families.

Table 12. Treatment of the Victims/Complainants at the Police Station at the Initial Stages

(i)	*Who Received the Complaint*	*Frequency*	*Percent*
(a)	Constable/Writer	59	54.6
(b)	Sub-Inspector	34	31.5
(c)	Inspector	15	13.9
	Total	108	100.0
(ii)	**Was the Complaint Received Immediately**		
(a)	Yes	96	88.9
(b)	No	12	11.1
	Total	108	100.0
(iii)	**Reasons For Delay in Reporting**		
(a)	Fear of secondary victimization by the accused	30	27.8
(b)	Tried to settle the issues within the family or	75	69.4
(c)	Other sources	3	2.8
	Total	108	100.0

With regard to monthly income, it was found that in 31.5% of the cases, the respondents earned upto Rs.500 a month; in 42.6% of the cases, the income was up to Rs. 1500; in 12.1% of the cases, they earned upto Rs. 2500 a month; in 4.6% of the cases, the monthly income was upto Rs. 3500 and in 9.2% of the cases, the respondents earned more than Rs. 3500 in a month.

When the respondents were asked as to who received their complaint at the police station, in 54.6% of the cases, the respondents said that their complaint was received by the Sub-Inspector and in the remaining 13.9% of the cases, the complaint was received by the Inspector of Police at the police station.

When asked if their complaint was received immediately, 88.9% of the respondents gave a positive reply whereas in the remaining 11.1% of the cases, the respondents were of the opinion that their complaint was not received immediately by the women police. The probable reason for this could be the non-availability of the women police at the station. With their limited strength they look after all the cases and some may have gone for other duties as a result they would not have been in the station when the victims/complainants approached the station in order to lodge a complaint.

When asked for the reasons for delay in the reporting of the incident, it was found that in 69.4% of the cases, the respondents opined that there was a delay in reporting of the crime because the problem being domestic in nature, they tried to settle the issue within the family. In 27.8% of the cases, the respondents said that the delay in the reporting behaviour was due to the fear of secondary victimization by the accused. In the remaining 2.8% of the cases, the delay in reporting on the part of the respondent was due to various other reasons such as fear of police, fear of family members etc.

The treatment of the victims/complainants at the police station by women police has been analysed individually with respect to the four districts, namely, Chennai, Villupuram, Kancheepuram and Vellore. The responses of the respondents regarding the treatment at the police station varied considerably in the four districts chosen for the present study.

The response to the question whether any care, sympathy or empathy was shown in taking down the complaint, was positive in all the four places. This is evident from the statistics given in the above table. In Chennai city, 82% of the respondents said that they were treated with care, sympathy and empathy and the percentage of positive reply in Villupuram, Kancheepuram and Vellore was 73.7%, 80% and 73.7% respectively. Of the total population, 18% of respondents in Chennai city, 26.3% in Villupuram, 20% in Kancheepuram and 26.3% in Vellore said that they were not treated with care, sympathy or empathy.

When asked if they were made to feel comfortable and consoled by the women police, 82% of the respondents in Chennai city, 73.7% in Villupuram, 85% in Kancheepuram and 73.7% in Vellore gave a positive reply. The remaining 18% of the respondents in Chennai, 26.3% in Villupuram, 15.5% in Kancheepuram

Table 13. Treatment of the Victims/Complainants at the Police Station

Sl. No	Nature of Accusation	Chennai			Villupuram			Kancheepuram			Vellore		
		Yes	No	NA	Yes	No	NA	Yes	No	NA	Yes	No	NA
		%	%	%	%	%	%	%	%	%	%	%	%
1	If any care, sympathy, empathy was shown in taking	82	18	-	73.7	26.3	-	80	20	-	73.7	26.3	-
2	If made to feel comfortable and consoled by women	82	18	-	73.7	26.3	-	85	15.5	-	73.7	26.3	-
3	If immediate action was taken by police on the receipt of	84	16	-	89.5	10.5	-	85	15.5	-	68.4	31.6	-
4	If police demanded any money/ compliment	20	80	-	36.8	63.2	-	25	75	-	5.3	94.7	-
5	If the police used any abusive language	8	92	-	15.8	84.2	-	5	95	-	36.8	63.2	-
6	If any preliminary enquiry was conducted by police	86	14	-	89.5	10.5	-	95	5	-	89.5	10.5	-
7	If the accused was arrested immediately	16	28	56	42.1	36.8	21.1	50	35	15	10.5	26.3	63.2
8	If the injuries were noted down by the police	14	4	82	10.5	5.3	84.2	10	10	80	10.5	-	89.5
9	If prompt medical attention was rendered	-	6	94	10.5	5.3	84.2	5	20	75	5.3	5.3	89.4
10	If police had advised for counselling	88	12	-	100	-	-	100	-	-	78.9	21.1	-
11	If First Information Report (FIR) was registered	6	94	-	36.8	63.2	-	75	25	-	31.6	68.4	-
12	If the accused was called to the station for enquiry	92	8	-	100	-	-	95	5	-	84.2	15.8	-
13	If the witnesses were called to the station for enquiry	78	22	-	94.7	5.3	-	100	-	-	78.9	21.1	-
14	If dowry articles were recovered and handed over	16	84	-	15.8	84.2	-	45	55	-	5.3	94.7	-
15	If effort was taken by the police to complete	72	28	-	78.9	21.1	-	85	15	-	73.7	26.3	-
16	If charge sheet was filed without delay	10	90	-	26.3	73.7	-	55	45	-	15.8	84.2	-
17	If the police rendered proper assistance to all	4	96	-	21.1	78.9	-	30	70	-	5.3	94.7	-
18	If there is any for pressure from any quarters to hush up	6	94	-	-	100	-	20	80	-	10.5	89.5	-
19	If any recommendation was needed for	60	40	-	47.4	52.6	-	30	70	-	21.1	78.9	-
20	If satisfied with the performance of women police	70	30	-	84.2	15.8	-	85	15	-	63.2	36.8	-

and 26.3% in Vellore district said that they were neither consoled nor made comfortable by the women police.

To the question if police took immediate action on receipt of their complaint, 84% of the respondents in Chennai city, 89.5% in Villupuram, 85% in Kancheepuram and 68.4% in Vellore district said that immediate action was taken by the women police on receipt of their complaint. Remaining 16% of the cases in Chennai, 10.5% in Villupuram, 15.5% in Kancheepuram and 31.6% in Vellore district felt that the women police on receipt of their complaint took no proper action. This dissatisfaction, in a small percentage of the sample, could be probably due to the fact that they would have given complaint against their husbands or in-laws etc. and would have demanded their immediate arrest. The reason for the dissatisfaction of a small percentage of the respondents may be due to the fact that the women police would have taken action only according to law and the given rules.

To the question if there was any demand of money or any other compliment by the police for taking action on their complaints, 20% the respondents in Chennai city, 36.8% in Villupuram, 25% in Kancheepuram and 5.3% in Vellore District gave a positive reply. In 80% of the cases in Chennai, 63.2% in Villupuram, 75% in Kancheepuram and 94.7% in Vellore districts said they were not demanded any money or any other compliment by the women police for taking action on their complaint.

On asking if the police used any abusive language when the complaint was given to them, 92% of the respondents in Chennai, 84.2% in Villupuram, 95% in Kancheepuram and 63.2% in Vellore district said that there was no such use of abusive language. However, 8% of the respondents in Chennai, 15.8% in Villupuram, 5% in Kancheepuram and 36.8% in Vellore district said that they had to listen to the abusive language of the women police while filing their complaint.

To the question whether any preliminary enquiry was conducted by the police in their case, the respondents replied favorably and this is evident from the statistics given in the above table. Kancheepuram district showed the highest percentage of positive response (95%) followed by Villupuram and Vellore districts with 89.5% and Chennai city with 86% of favourable response. Only 14% of the respondents in Chennai, 10.5% in Villupuram, 5% in Kancheepuram and 10.5% in Vellore district said that no preliminary enquiry was done in their case. This could probably be due to the nature of offence. In the case of a serious offence, the First Information Register (FIR) is registered and the accused is arrested immediately. No preliminary enquiry is conducted in such cases.

When asked if the accused was arrested immediately, 84% of respondents in Chennai, 57.9% in Villupuram, 50% in Kancheepuram and 89.5% in Vellore district said that the accused was not immediately arrested by the police. However, in 16% of the cases in Chennai, 42% in Villupuram, 50% in Kancheepuram and 10.5% in Vellore district, the respondents said that the accused was arrested immediately by the women police.

A majority of the cases normally dealt by the women police pertain to family disputes, marital maladjustments, harassments etc. Most of the complaints are made against the husbands or other in-laws. Normally, in such cases, the accused is not arrested immediately by the women police. There is a preliminary enquiry conducted and the families are counselled by the women police. Only in cases of cognizable offence, the accused is immediately arrested by the women police or any other serious matter which warranted a prima facie case called for the immediate arrest of the accused.

When asked if their injuries were noted down by the police, 86% of the respondents in Chennai, 89.5% in Villupuram, 90% in Kancheepuram and 89.5% in Vellore district said that no attention was paid by the women police to the injuries sustained by them. Only in 14% of the cases in Chennai, 10.5% in Villupuram, 10% in Kancheepuram and 10.5% in Vellore said that their injuries were noted down by the police.

In 100% of the cases in Chennai, 89.5% in Villupuram, 95% in Kanchepuram and 94.8% in Vellore district, the victims were neither given any kind of medical attention nor did the police take them to any hospital. Only in 10.5% of cases in Villupuram, 5% in Kancheepuram and 5.3% in Vellore districts, they were paid some medical attention by the police.

However, the response to the question whether the police had advised the victims/complainants counselling, was quite favourable in all the four places. All the respondents in Villupuram and Kancheepuram replied that they had received counselling by the women police and the percentage in Chennai and Vellore was 88 and 78.9 respectively. Only 12% of the respondents in Chennai city and 21% in Vellore district said that they did not receive any advice for counselling by the women police.

Counselling is usually done by the women police in the cases of family disputes, quarrels with in-laws, marital maladjustment etc. In the cases where the First Information Report (FIR) is registered, no counselling is given by the women police to the victims/ complainants.

When asked if the First Information Report (FIR) was registered immediately by the police after the complaint was received, 94% of the respondents in Chennai, 63.1% in Villupuram, 25% in Kancheepuram and 68.4% in Vellore district gave a negative reply. Only 6% of the respondents in Chennai, 36.8% in Villupuram, 75% in Kancheepuram and 31.6% in Vellore district said that the First Information Report (FIR) was registered immediately after filing a complaint. The cases usually dealt with by the women police pertain to family disputes, domestic violence etc. Hence in most of the cases, they try to settle the issue by counselling/advice. Only in the cases where the offence is of a serious nature warranting a prima facie case, the First Information Report (FIR) is registered immediately by the women police.

To a question if the accused was called to the police station for enquiry, 92% of the respondents in Chennai, 100% in Villupuram, 95% in Kancheepuram and 84.2%

in Vellore district answered positively and said that the police had called the accused to the station for enquiry. However, in 8% of cases in Chennai, 5% in Kancheepuram and 15.8% in Vellore district said that the accused was not called to the station for enquiry.

The accused in cases of domestic violence etc. can either be males or females. In cases where the accused is a female, they are usually not called to the police station for enquiry by the police. Similarly, if the accused is an aged person, he is not called to the station for the purpose of enquiry. Sometimes, the police might settle the issue by counselling. In such cases also, the accused is not called to the police station for enquiry by the women police.

On asking if the witnesses were called to the police station for enquiry, 78% of the respondents in Chennai, 94.7% in Villupuram, 100% in Kancheepuram and 78.9% in Vellore district answered positively whereas 22% in Chennai, 5.3% in Villupuram and 21% in Vellore district replied that the witnesses were not called by the police for any enquiry.

In the cases of witnesses also, women and the aged are not usually called to the station for the purpose of enquiry. Sometimes, the witnesses refuse to come to the police station and plead ignorance so as to escape from the situation. In such cases, it becomes difficult to get these people to the police station for enquiry.

When asked if their dowry articles were recovered and handed over to them, it is regrettable to note that in 84% of the cases in Chennai, 84.2% in Villupuram, 55% in Kancheepuram and 94.7% in Vellore district, the respondents said that their dowry articles were neither recovered nor handed over to them by the police whereas in 16% of cases in Chennai, 15.8% in Villupuram, 45% in Kancheepuram and 5.3% in Vellore district, the respondents said that their articles were recovered and handed over to them by the police.

Most of the cases that come to the women police stations are counselled and settled by them as they are usually the cases of family disputes, domestic violence etc. Hence in those situations, the need for recovering the dowry articles does not arise.

It is interesting to note that in 72% of the cases in Chennai, 78.9% in Villupuram, 85% in Kancheepuram and 73% in Vellore district, the respondents said that care and effort was taken by the police to complete the investigation at the earliest. Only 28% of respondents in Chennai, 21.1% in Villupuram, 15% in Kancheepuram and 16.3% in Vellore district replied negatively and said that no proper effort was taken by the women police to complete the investigation at the earliest.

When asked if the chargesheet was filed without any delay, 90% of the respondents in Chennai, 73.7% in Villupuram, 45% in Kancheepuram and 84.2% in Vellore district said that there was delay in filing the chargesheet. Only 10% of respondents in Chennai, 26.3% in Villupuram, 55% in Kancheepuram and 15.8% in Vellore district said that there was no delay in filing a chargesheet in their case.

The delay in filing a chargesheet against the accused could probably be due to the treatment of the case as a petition enquiry. At times, the case would have been dropped after registration and during enquiry. In other cases, the police would have settled the matter by counselling or advice or in some cases, there may be a case of mistake of fact due to exaggeration by witnesses or victims/complainants. Hence, there would have been a delay in filing a chargesheet against the accused.

On asking if the police rendered proper assistance to the witnesses for deposing before the court, 96% of the respondents in Chennai, 78.9% in Villupuram, 70% in Kancheepuram and 94.7% in Vellore district said that no such assistance was rendered to the witnesses whereas in 4% of the cases in Chennai city, 21.1% in Villupuram, 30% in Kancheepuram and 5.3% in Vellore district said that the witnesses were given proper assistance by the police for making deposition before the court.

Usually, the witnesses go to the court directly to give evidence when summoned by the court. So no assistance in the form of vehicles etc. is provided by the police to the witnesses. If the police take the witnesses to the court, then the defence blames the police for having foisted the witness in their favour. Only in the cases where there is a threat to the life of the witnesses by the accused or where the witness goes to the police station for refreshing memory, the police provide assistance to the witness for appearing before the court.

When asked if there was any pressure from any of the quarters to hush up the case, 94% of the respondents in Chennai city, 100% in Villupuram, 80% in Kancheepuram and 89.5% in Vellore district said that there was no such pressure from anywhere but 6% of the respondents in Chennai, 20% in Kancheepuram and 10.5% in Vellore district confirmed the presence of such pressure to hush up the case.

When asked if any recommendation was needed to follow up the case, 60% of the respondents in Chennai, 47.4% in Villupuram, 30% in Kancheepuram and 21.1% in Vellore district said that there was a need for recommendation to follow up their case. However, in 40% of the cases in Chennai, 52.6% in Villupuram, 70% in Kancheepuram and 78.9% in Vellore district, the respondents were of the opinion that there was no need for any recommendation for the follow up of their case.

Recommendations would be needed only in those cases where the victims/complainants want to end their case at the earliest and hence for speedier investigation, would have gone for recommendation. Also, in cases where the victims/complainants are illiterates and are scared to go to the police station, they may seek the help of influential persons to follow up their case and to know the proceedings of the case.

To the question if they were satisfied with the performance of the women police in their cases, it is heartening to note that 70% of the respondents in Chennai city, 84.2% in Villupuram, 85% in

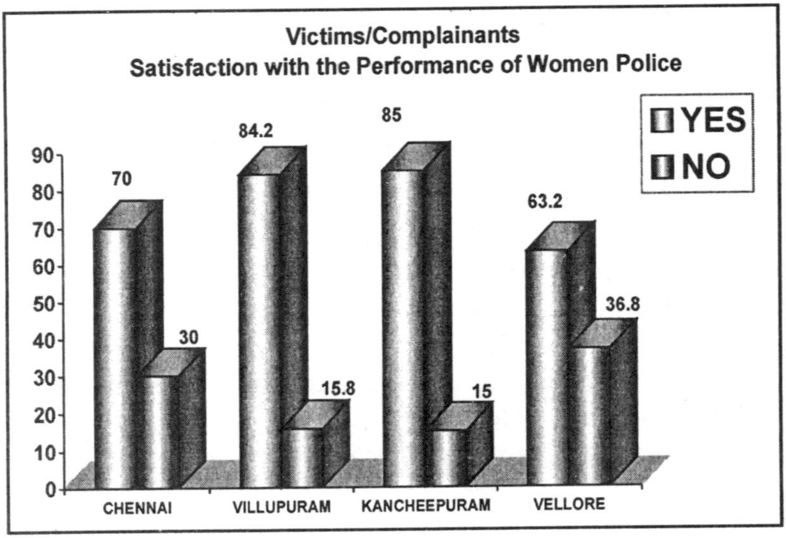

Fig. 5.

Kancheepuram and 63.2% in Vellore district said that they were happy with the performance of the women police in their case whereas in 30% of cases in Chennai, 15.8% in Villpuram, 15% in Kancheepuram and 36.8% in Vellore District, the respondents showed some dissatisfaction with regard to the performance of the women police in their case.

A small percentage of dissatisfaction on the part of victims/complainants arises from the negligence on the part of the police, indifference of the police and delay in taking action.

Methods of Treatment of the Witnesses by Women Police in Tamil Nadu

The given table explains the bio-demographic characteristics of the witnesses.

Table 14. Profile of the Witnesses

Sl. No.		Frequency	Percent
1.	**Age**		
	18-28 years	8	11.2
	29-38 years	10	14.0
	39-48 years	19	26.6
	49-58 years	16	22.5
	Above 58 years	18	25.2
	Total	71	100.0
2.	**Sex**		
	Male	34	47.9
	Female	37	52.1
	Total	71	100.0
3.	**Marital Status**		
	Married	57	80.3
	Unmarried	2	2.8
	Widow	11	15.5
	Separated	1	1.4
	Total	71	100.0
4.	**Religion**		
	Hindu	58	81.7
	Muslim	7	9.9
	Christian	6	8.4
	Total	71	100.0
5.	**Nativity**		
	Rural	45	63.4
	Urban	26	36.6
	Total	71	100.0

From the above table, it is evident that in 11.2.% of the cases, the respondents were in the age group between 18-28 years; 14% in the age group between 29-38 years; 26.6% between 39-48 years, 22.5% between 49-58 years and the remaining 25.2% of the respondents were above 58 years of age.

52.1% of the respondents were females and 47.9% of the respondents were males.

80.3% of the respondents were married, 15.5% widows, 2.8% unmarried and the remaining 1.4% of the respondents were living separately and were not with their spouses.

81.7% of the respondents belonged to Hinduism; 9.9% were Muslims and 8.4% of the respondents were Christians.

Table 15. Profile of Witnesses

Sl. No.		Frequency	Percent
1.	**Education**		
	Illiterate	34	47.9
	Upto 5th Standard	18	25.4
	Upto 10th Standard	16	22.5
	Under Graduate	2	2.8
	Post Graduate	1	1.4
	Total	71	100.0
2.	**Occupation**		
	Housewife	5	7.0
	Housemaid	19	26.8
	Daily Wage Earner	32	45.1
	Office	10	14.1
	Business	5	7.0
	Total	71	100.0
3.	**Monthly Income**		
	Upto Rs.500	20	28.2
	Rs.501- Rs.1500	29	40.8
	Rs.1501- Rs.2500	11	15.5
	Rs.2501- Rs.3500	5	7.0
	Above Rs.3500	6	8.5
	Total	71	100.0
4.	**Nature Of Family**		
	Joint	30	42.3
	Nuclear	41	57.7
	Total	71	100.0

As far as the nativity of respondents was concerned, 63.4% of the respondents hailed from rural areas and in the remaining 36.6% of the cases, the respondents hailed from urban areas.

As far as the educational qualification of the respondents was concerned, 47.9% of the respondents were illiterates; 25.4% had obtained education upto 5th standard; 22.5% of them had obtained education upto 10th standard; 2.8% of them were graduates and the remaining 1.4% of the respondents had obtained their post graduate degree.

As far as the monthly income of the respondents was concerned, it is evident from the table that in 40.8% of the cases, the respondents earned upto Rs.1500 in a month. In 28.2% of the cases, they earned upto Rs.500 a month; 15.5% earned between Rs. 1501- Rs. 2500; 7% of the respondents earned between Rs. 2501–Rs. 3500 and the remaining 8.5% of the respondents earned more than Rs. 3500 a month.

As far as the occupation of the respondents was concerned, 45.1 % of the respondents worked as coolies, 26.8% of them, earned their living by doing house hold work as housemaids, 14.1% were office goers, 7% were in business and the remaining 7% were unemployed.

The given table explains the relationship of the witnesses with the victims/ complainants. In a vast majority of the cases (95.8%), the respondents were the relatives of the victims/complainants. In 2.8% of the cases they happened to be the neighbours and in the remaining 1.4% of the cases, the respondents happened to be friends of the victims/complainants. Since a

Table 16. Relationship of Witnesses with Victims/Complainants/ Accused

Sl. No.		Frequency	Percent
1.	Relationship with Victims/Complainants		
	Friends	1	1.4
	Neighbour	2	2.8
	Relative	68	95.8
	Total	71	100.0
2.	Relationship with Accused		
	No Relationship	4	5.6
	Friends	1	1.4
	Neighbour	2	2.8
	Relative	64	90.2
	Total	71	100.0

majority of the cases dealt with by the women police were pertaining to family disputes, domestic violence, maladjustment, harassment etc. the witnesses obviously happened to be near relatives of the victims/ complainants such as father, sister, mother etc.

The respondents also shared a relationship with the accused. The above table suggested that in 90.2% of the cases, the respondents were relatives of the accused; in 5.6% of the cases, they did not share any relationship with the accused; in 2.8% of the cases, the respondents were the neighbours of the accused and in the remaining 1.4% of the cases, the respondents were the friends of the accused.

Table 17. The Reception at the Police Station by Women Police when called for Enquiry

Sl. No.		Chennai	Villupuram	Kancheepuram	Vellore
1.	Poor	60.9%	83.3%	40%	6.7%
2.	Good	26.1%	5.6%	46.7%	53.3%
3.	Satisfactory	13%	11.1%	13.3%	40%

When asked about their reception at the police station, 60.9% of the respondents in Chennai city said that the reception at the police station was poor and this was seen in 83.3% of the cases in Villupuram, 40% in Kancheepuram and 6.7% in Vellore district. In 26.1% cases in Chennai city, 5.6% in Villupuram, 46.7% in Kancheepuram and 53.3% in Vellore, the respondents found their reception good. In the remaining 13% of cases in Chennai city, 11.1% in Villupuram, 13.3% in Kancheepuram and 40% in Vellore, the respondents found their reception at the police station satisfactory.

The table reveals that there were respondents who felt that their reception at the police station was poor. The reasons for this opinion could be that they would not have been offered a place to sit when the enquiry was being conducted in the police station due to lack of infra structural facilities or may be the concerned officer would have gone out for some case and the witnesses would have waited for a long time at the police station.

This section deals with the treatment given to the witnesses by the women police at the police station. The United Nations Declaration on Basic Principles of Justice for Victims of Crime and Abuse of Power (1985) expects that all victims and witnesses should be treated with compassion, respect and dignity. This section analyses the treatment rendered to the witnesses by the women police at the police station in the four districts, namely Chennai, Villupuram, Kancheepuram and Vellore.

Table 18. Treatment of the witnesses by Women Police at the Police Station

Sl. No	Nature of Accusation	Chennai		Villupuram		Kanchee - Puram		Vellore	
		Yes	No	Yes	No	Yes	No	Yes	No
		%	%	%	%	%	%	%	%
1	If treated with dignity respect, politeness, kindness, sympathy and empathy	91.3	8.7	83.3	16.7	73.7	26.7	73.3	26.7
2	If women police used any abusive language during investigation	17.4	82.6	38.9	61.1	20	80	33.3	66.7
3	If women police performed their duty fairly	78.3	21.7	83.3	16.7	80	20	73.3	26.7
4	If women police performed their duty legally	39.1	60.9	83.3	16.7	80	20	80	20
5	If they felt comfortable at the police station during enquiry	91.3	8.7	83.3	16.7	80	20	66.7	33.3
6	If forced by women police to depose evidence	8.7	91.3	16.7	83.3	13.3	86.7	6.7	93.3
7	If asked to give money or other compliments to the women police	26.1	73.9	22.2	77.8	26.7	73.3	6.7	93.3
8	If women police handle the women issues better than men.	78.3	21.7	83.3	16.7	80	20	73.3	26.7

It is interesting to note that in majority of the cases in the present study when the witnesses were asked if they were treated with dignity, respect, politeness, kindness, sympathy and empathy, there was a positive response. 91.3% of the respondents in Chennai city, 83.3% in Villupuram, 73.7% in Kancheepuram and 73.3% in Vellore district said that they were given a sympathetic and kind treatment by the women police.

In Kancheepuram and Vellore, 26.7% respondents said that they did not get a fair treatment from the police.

When asked if the women police used any abusive language during the course of investigation 17.4% of the respondents in Chennai, 38.9% in Villupuram, 20% in Kancheepuram and 33.3% in Vellore district were of the opinion that there was indulgence of abusive languages on the part of the police during the course of investigation. In 82.6% of the cases in Chennai, 61.1% in Villupuram, 80% in Kancheepuram 66.7% in Vellore district, the respondents opined that the police did not use any abusive language.

Regarding the performance of women police, 78.3% of the respondents in Chennai City, 83.3% in Villupuram, 80% in Kancheepuram and 73.3% in Vellore found the performance of women police fair and satisfactory whereas the remaining 21.7% of the respondents in Chennai, 16.7% in Villupuram, 20% in Kancheepuam and 26.7% in Vellore felt that the performance of the women police was not satisfactory.

When asked if the women police performed their duties lawfully, 39.1% of the respondents in Chennai, 83.3% in Villupuram, 80% in Kancheepuram and Vellore district gave an affirmative response. The remaining 60.9% of the respondents in Chennai, 16.7% in Villupuram and 20% in Kancheepuram and Vellore opined that the women police did not really perform their duties lawfully.

Normally, the cases are filed or registered by the police only if it is a cognizable one. If the women police are of the opinion that the matter can be settled through counselling, then the complaint is not registered. Only in serious cases or in cases of cognizable offence, a complaint is registered by the police. The respondents on the other hand want their cases to be registered if the victim is their relative. When this does not happen, they feel that the women police are not performing their duties legally.

Here again, the opinion depends upon the level of satisfaction of the respondents of the women police. If the action of the police results in benefits to the respondents, then they feel satisfied. On the contrary, if the action of the women police does not produce any benefit or desirable results, it leads to dissatisfaction of the respondents. For e.g., the respondents would have demanded immediate action on the accused in case the victim involved is their relative even if it was a non-cognizable offence. When this does not happen, they feel that the women police are partial in conducting their case.

When asked if they felt comfortable at the police station during enquiry, 91.3% of the respondents in Chennai, 83.3% in Villupuram, 80% in Kancheepuram and 66.7% in Vellore district were of the opinion that they felt comfortable at the police station during enquiry whereas the remaining 8.7% of the respondents in Chennai, 16.7% in Villupuram, 20% in Kancheepuram and 33.3% in Vellore district opined that they were not really comfortable at the police station during the enquiry. The probable reasons for a small percentage of the respondents to feel uncomfortable could be due to the poor infrastructural facilities at the police station, long waiting hours during enquiry, fear of the police, lack of public utility facilities etc. The respondents would have been made to wait at the police station for long hours or they would not have been offered a place to sit at the station or the police being engaged in their regular work would not have paid attention, which might have made a small percentage of the respondents uncomfortable at the police station.

On asking if they were forced by the police to depose evidence, 91.3% of the respondents in Chennai, 83.3% in Villupuram, 86.7% in Kancheepuram and 93.3% in Vellore district opined that there was no such force inflicted by the women police on them whereas the remaining 8.7% of the respondents in Chennai, 16.7% in Villupuram, 13.3% in Kancheepuram and 6.7% in Vellore said that they had been forced by the women police to depose evidence in the way the police wanted them to.

When asked if they were asked to give money or any other compliments to the women police, 73.9% respondents in Chennai, 77.8% in Villupuram, 73.3% in Kancheepuram and 93.3% in Vellore district said that they were not asked to pay any money or other compliments to the police whereas in the remaining 26.1% cases in Chennai, 22.2% in Villurpuram, 26.7% in Kancheepuram and 6.7% in Vellore district, the respondents said that they had to pay money or other compliments to the women police.

It is interesting to note that when the respondents were asked if the women police handled issues concerning women better than the men, 78.3% of the respondents in Chennai, 83.3% in Villupuram, 80% in Kancheepuram and 73.3% in Vellore district gave a positive response; whereas the remaining 21.7% of the respondents in Chennai, 16.7% in Villupuram, 20% in Kancheepuram and 26.7% in Vellore district were of the opinion that the women police did not handle the issues relating to women in a satisfactory manner when compared to men.

Methods of Treatment of the Accused by Women Police in Tamil Nadu

Table 19. Profile of the accused

SL. No.		*Frequency*	*Percent*
1.	**Age**		
	21-30 Years	22	38.6
	31-40 Years	23	40.4
	41-50 Years	7	12.3
	Above 58 Years	5	8.7
	Total	57	100.0
2.	**Sex**		
	Male	50	87.7
	Female	7	12.3
	Total	57	100.0
3.	**Marital Status**		
	Married	47	82.5
	Unmarried	3	5.3
	Divorced	1	1.7
	Widow	1	1.7
	Separated	5	8.8
	Total	57	100.0
4.	**Religion**		
	Hindu	49	86.0
	Muslim	4	7.0
	Christian	4	7.0
	Total	57	100.0
5.	**Nativity**		
	Rural	35	61.4
	Urban	22	38.6
	Total	57	100.0

The above table gives the profile of the accused such as age, sex, martial status, nativity etc.

From the above table, it is evident that in 38.6% of the cases, the respondents fall in the age group between 21-30 years, 40.4% between 31-40 years, 12.3% fall in the age group between 41-50 years and the remaining 8.7% of the respondents are above 50 years of age. 87.7% of the respondents chosen for the present study are males and the remaining 12.3% of the respondents are females. In 82.5% of the cases, the respondents are married, 5.3% are unmarried, 8.8% are separated from their spouses, 1.7% are widows and the remaining 1.7% of the respondents are divorced. In a vast majority of the cases (86%), the respondents belong to Hinduism and an equal percentage of the respondents (7%) are Muslims and Christians.

With regard to the nativity of the respondents, in 61.4% of the cases, the respondents hail from rural areas whereas in the remaining 38.6% of the cases, the respondents hail from urban areas.

Table 20. Profile of Accused

SL. No.		*Frequency*	*Percent*
1.	**Education**		
	Illiterate	19	33.3
	Upto 5th Standard	10	17.5
	Upto 10th Standard	17	29.8
	Upto 12th Standard	5	8.8
	Under Graduate	4	7.0
	Post Graduate	2	3.5
	Total	57	100.0

(contd.)

SL. No.		Frequency	Percent
2.	**Occupation:**		
	No job	2	3.5
	Housemaid	5	8.8
	Daily Wage Earner	37	64.9
	Office	3	5.3
	Business	6	10.5
	Professional	4	7.0
	Total	57	100.0
3.	**Monthly Income**		
	Upto Rs.500	14	24.7
	Rs.501- Rs.1500	29	51.0
	Rs.1501- Rs.2500	7	12.3
	Rs.2501- Rs.3500	2	3.5
	Above Rs.3500	5	8.5
	Total	57	100.0
4.	**Nature Of Family**		
	Joint	26	45.6
	Nuclear	31	54.4
	Total	57	100.0

The above table explains the demographic characteristics of the respondents. As evident from the table, in 33.3% of the cases, the respondents are illiterates, 17.5% have obtained education upto 5th standard, 29.8% have completed 10th standard, 8.8% have passed their 12th standard, 7% are graduates and the remaining 3.5% of the respondents have obtained their post graduation degree.

With regard to the occupational status of the respondents, it is evident from the table that a majority of the respondents (64.9%) work as coolies, 10.5% are into business, 7% are professionals, 8.8% work as house maids, 5.3% of the respondents are office goers and the remaining 3.5% of the respondents are unemployed.

With respect to the monthly income of the respondents, in 24.7% of the cases, the respondents earn upto Rs. 500 a month; in 51% of the cases, the monthly income of the respondents is between Rs. 501-1500; in 12.3% of the cases, the respondents earn between Rs. 1501-2500 a month; in 3.5% of the cases, the respondents earn upto Rs. 3500 a month and in the remaining 8.5% of the cases, the respondents earn more than Rs. 3500 a month.

With regard to the nativity of the respondents, it is evident from the table that in 45.6% of the cases, the respondents live in joint families whereas in the remaining 54.4% of the cases, the respondents live in a nuclear family.

Table 12. Offence of the accused

Offence of The Accused	*Chennai*		*Villupuram*		*Kancheepuram*		*Vellore*	
	F	%	F	%	F	%	F	%
Family Dispute	14	77.8	8	72.7	2	15.4	1	6.6
Dowry Demand	-	-	-	-	6	46.2	4	26.7
Ill-treatment of Wife	3	16.6	-	-	1	7.6	3	20.0
Marital Maladjustment	1	5.6	-	-	2	15.4	3	20.0
Other reasons	-	-	3	27.3	2	15.4	4	26.7

The first table elicits the nature of offence committed by the accused. In the city of Chennai, in 77.8% of the cases, the nature of accusation is domestic violence. As far as Villupuram district is concerned, 72.7% of the cases are related to family disputes and the remaining 27.3% of the cases are other than dowry demand, ill-treatment of wife, marital maladjustment etc. In the district of Kancheepuram, the majority (46.2%) of the cases are pertaining to dowry demand. As far as Vellore district is concerned, 6.6% of them are pertaining to family disputes, 26.7% of the cases are of dowry demand, 20% of the cases are pertaining to ill-treatment of wife and another 20% of the cases are of marital maladjustment while the remaining 26.7% of the cases are of other categories.

Table 22. Treatment at the time of Arrest

Sl. No	*Nature of Accusation*	*Chennai*		*Villupuram*		*Kanchee - Puram*		*Vellore*	
		Yes	*No*	*Yes*	*No*	*Yes*	*No*	*Yes*	*No*
		%	%	%	%	%	%	%	%
1	If called for counselling at the police station before arrest	22.2	77.8	63.6	36.4	53.8	46.2	20	80
2	If informed the reasons for arrest	16.7	83.3	63.6	36.4	38.5	61.6	-	100
3	If produced before appropriate court within 24 hours of the arrest	-	100	27.3	72.8	38.5	61.6	6.6	93.4
4	If hand -cuffed at the time of arrest	-	100	18.2	81.8	7.7	92.3	-	100
5	If the p olice officer effected the arrest was in uniform	11.1	88.9	36.3	63.7	76.9	23.1	6.7	93.3

When asked if they were called to the police station for counselling before the arrest, 22.2% of the respondents in Chennai, 63.6% in Villupuram, 53.8% in Kancheepuram and 20% of the respondents in Vellore said that they were called for a counselling session at the police station before the arrest. Nevertheless, 77.8% of the respondents in Chennai, 36.4% in Villupuram, 46.2% in Kancheepuram and 80% of the respondents in

Vellore district said that they were not called for any sort of counselling before the arrest at the police station. Counselling is given only in cases of family disputes etc. where the problem is not of a serious nature and can be settled through counselling. In cases of cognizable offences, the accused is arrested immediately and is not given any counselling. The accused were asked if they had been informed about the reason of their arrest by the women police. It is surprising to note that in 83.3% of the cases in Chennai, 36.4% in Villupuram, 61.6% in Kancheepuram and 100% of the cases in Vellore district, the respondents were not informed about the reason of their arrest by the women police. In the remaining 16.7% of the cases in Chennai, 63.6% in Villupuram and 38.5% in Kancheepuram, the accused were informed about the grounds on which they were arrested.

When asked whether they were produced before the appropriate court within 24 hours of their arrest, 100% of the respondents in Chennai, 72.8% in Villupuram, 61.6% in Kancheepuram and 93.4% of the respondents in Vellore district said that they were not produced before the appropriate courts within 24 hours of their arrest. 27.3% of the respondents in Villupuram, 38.5% in Kancheepuram and 6.6% of the respondents in Vellore district opined that they were presented before the appropriate court within 24 hours of their arrest. As explained earlier, the respondents were arrested only in cases of cognizable offence. When the accused is arrested, he may be sent on bail or he may be remanded etc. after he is produced before the magistrate.

The accused were asked if they were handcuffed at the time of arrest. In 100% of the cases in Chennai and Vellore, 81.8% of the cases in Villupuram and 92.3% of the cases in Kancheepuram district, the respondents said that they were not handcuffed by the women police. However, a meagre 18.2% of the respondents in Villupuram district and 6.7% in Vellore district opined that they were handcuffed by the women police at the time of their arrest. As per the guidelines given by the Supreme Court in D.K. Basu's case, no accused should be handcuffed except under certain circumstances. Following the guidelines, the accused are normally not handcuffed by the women police except in cases where the accused is very violent in nature or where he tries to defy the orders of the police or where there are all chances of his escaping from the clutches of law etc. When asked if the police officer who effected the arrest was in uniform, 88.9% of the respondents in Chennai, 63.7% in Villupuram, 23.1% in Kancheepuram and 93.3% in Vellore district said that the police officer who effected the arrest was not in uniform. However, in remaining 11.1% of the cases in Chennai, 36.3% in Villupuram, 76.9% of the cases in Kancheepuram and 6.7% of the cases in Vellore district, the respondents said that the police officer who arrested them was in uniform. The women police are given the permission to carry out the arrest even in civil clothes provided they carry their identity cards with them as in certain cases, the accused might try to escape seeing the police women in uniform. Hence in certain cases, they are permitted to perform their duties even if they are not in their uniforms.

Table 23. Treatment of the accused at the Police Station

Sl. No	Nature of Accusation	Chennai		Villupuram		Kanchee - Puram		Vellore	
		Yes	No	Yes	No	Yes	No	Yes	No
		%	%	%	%	%	%	%	%
1.	If arrest was informed to their relatives	5.6	94.4	54.5	45.5	53.8	46.2	6.7	93.3
2.	If provided proper food at the police station during custody	-	100	18.1	81.9	61.5	38.5	6.7	93.3
3.	If the police tried to settle the issue through counselling/advice	50	50	63.6	36.4	61.5	38.5	26.7	73.3
4.	If attempt of police officer to settle the domestic issue was successful	66.7	33.3	72.7	27.3	53.8	46.2	46.7	53.3
5.	If prompt medical assistance was given on request	33.3	66.7	9.1	90.9	23.1	76.9	6.7	93.3
6.	If permitted to meet lawyer at any time during interrogation	-	100	18.2	81.8	53.8	46.2	13.3	86.7
7.	If subjected to physical torture during interrogation at the police station	-	100	36.3	63.7	23.1	76.9	-	100
8.	If verbally abused during interrogation	-	100	27.3	72.7	30.8	69.2	6.7	93.3
9.	If women police demanded money to do things in your favour	16.7	83.3	27.3	72.7	15.4	84.6	13.3	86.7

This section throws light on the treatment given to the accused by the women police at the police station in Chennai City, Villupuram, Kancheepuram and Vellore districts.

The accused were asked if their arrest was informed to their relatives. In 94.4% of the cases in Chennai City, 45.5% in Villupuram, 46.2% in Kancheepuram and 93.3% of the cases in Vellore district the respondents said that their arrest was not informed to their relatives. However, in 5.6% of the cases in Chennai, 54.5% in Villupuram, 53.8% in Kancheepuram and 6.7% of the cases in Vellore district, the respondents said that their relatives were informed.

When asked if they were provided with proper food at the police station during custody, all the cases (100%)

in Chennai, 81.9% of the cases in Villupuram, 38.5% in Kancheepuram and 93.3% of the cases in Vellore district gave a negative response and said that they were not provided with proper food at the police station during custody. In the remaining 18.2% of the respondents in Villupuram district, 61.5% in Kancheepuram and 6.7% of the respondents in Vellore district said that they were provided with proper food at the police station during custody.

It must be noted that in certain cases the accused once arrested might be released on bail. In that case, there is no need to provide him with food. Similarly in cases where the accused is arrested but released immediately or cases where the accused is promptly produced before the court etc. there is no need of providing him with food during custody.

The respondents were asked if the police tried to settle the issue through counselling / advice after their arrest. In 50% of the cases in Chennai, 63.6% in Villupuram 61.5% in Kancheepuram and 26.7% of the cases in Vellore district, the respondents said that the police tried to settle the issue through counselling / advice after their arrest. However, in 50% of the cases in Chennai, 36.4% in Villupuram, 38.5% in Kancheepuram and 73.3% in Vellore district, the respondents gave a negative response. Normally, counselling is given by the women police only in the cases that are of a petty nature. In such cases, the police tries to settle the issue through counselling/advice. As far as the cases of cognizable offences are concerned, the police do not try to settle the issue through counselling/advice, the First Information Register (FIR) is immediately registered by the police.

When asked if the attempt to settle the domestic issue by the police officer was successful, it is interesting to note that in 66.7% of the cases in Chennai, 72.7% in Villupuram, 53.8% in Kancheepuram and 46.7% of the cases in Vellore district, the respondents gave a positive response where as in the remaining 33.3% of the cases in Chennai, 27.3% in Villupuram, 46.2% in Kancheepurm and 53.3% of the cases in Vellore district, the respondents were of the opinion that the attempt made by the police officer to settle the domestic issue was not successful.

When asked if they were permitted to meet their lawyer at any time during interrogation, 100% of the respondents in Chennai, 81.8.% in Villupuram, 46.2% in Kancheepuram and 86.7% of the respondents in Vellore district gave a negative response and said that they were not permitted to meet their lawyer during interrogation whereas in the remaining 18.2% of the cases in Villupuram, 53.8% in Kancheepuram and 13.3% of the cases in Vellore district, the respondents opined that they were permitted to meet their lawyer at the time of interrogation. There are certain cases where the accused does not really need a lawyer at the time of interrogation by the police. Also, when there are possibilities of the accused tampering with the case, then, the lawyer is not allowed to sit with the accused at the time of interrogation by the police.

As far as the question of physical torture during interrogation by the women police at the police station is concerned, 100% of the respondents in Chennai, 63.7% in Villupuram 76.9% in Kancheepuram and 100% of the respondents in Vellore district said that they were not subjected to any kind of torture by women police during interrogation at the police station whereas in the remaining 36.3% of the cases in Villupuram and 23.1% of the cases in Kancheepuram district, the respondents opined that they were subjected to torture by the women police at the police station during interrogation.

When asked if there was any verbal abuse by the women police during interrogation, in 100% of the cases in Chennai, 72.7% in Villupuram, 69.2% in Kancheepuram and 93.3% of the cases in Vellore district, the respondents said that they were not abused verbally during interrogation by the women police whereas in 27.3% of cases in Villupuram, 30.8% in Kancheepuram and 6.7% of the cases in Vellore district, the respondents said that they were verbally abused by women police during interrogation at the police station.

As far as the demand of money by the women police is concerned, 83.3% of the respondents in Chennai, 72.7% in Villupuram, 84.6% in Kancheepuram and 86.7% of the respondents in Vellore district said that there was no demand for any money by the women police to do things in their favour. However, in 16.7% of the cases in Chennai, 27.3% in Villupuram 15.4% in Kancheepuram and 13.3% of the cases in Vellore district, the respondents said that there was a demand for money by the women police to do things in their favour.

5

Comparative Analysis

HYPOTHESIS

Women Police

(i) There will be no association between the education of the respondents.

(a) their opinion of their job with respect to choosing police work as career, if police job is better than other jobs etc.

(b) the opinion of the family and society i.e. appreciation by family and friends, co-operation of husband and in-laws etc.

(c) the recognition in society.

(d) their working conditions.

(e) the welfare measures.

(ii) There will be no association between the nativity of the respondents.

(a) their opinion of their job with respect to choosing police work as a career, if police job is better than other jobs etc.

(b) the opinion of the family and society i.e. appreciation by family and friends, co-operation of husband and in-laws etc.

(c) the recognition in society.

(d) their working conditions.

(e) their job satisfaction.

(iii) There will be no association between the rank of the respondents.

(a) their opinion of their job with respect to choosing police work as a career, if police job is better than other jobs etc.

(b) the opinion of the family and society i.e. appreciation by family and friends, co-operation of husband and in-laws etc.

(c) the reaction of the in-laws with respect to working with men.

(d) their working conditions.

(e) their job satisfaction.

(iv) There will be no association between the number of working hours and the co-operation of their family i.e. husband, in-laws, opinion of working with men etc.

(v) There will be no association between the working conditions of the respondents and their age.

The responses of the respondents to questions with regard to choosing police work as career, whether police job was better than other jobs, whether the job suits their ability or whether they will continue to work till retirement, had no significant association to their educational qualification.

Table 1. Association between Education of the Respondents and their Opinion of their Job

Variable	x^2 *Value*	*Significance*
Choosing Police work as career	10.14006	0.11888
If Police job is better than other departments	0.19416	0.90748
If the job suits their ability	0.33084	0.84754
Will continue work till retirement	1.11393	0.57294

The respondents choose police job because of the job security, monetary benefits etc. The education does not play any major role in selecting the police job.

Similarly, a policewoman may hold the opinion that the police job is better than the ones in other departments. On the other hand another policewoman may opine otherwise. There may be so many reasons for this, such as job satisfaction, police powers or working conditions, etc. Any one of these could be the reasons for a policewoman to believe that the police job is the best or even otherwise. Nevertheless, the education of the respondent does not associate with the opinion.

To the question if the job suited their ability, a majority of the respondents opined that the job did suit their ability. The results also indicate that there is no significant association between their level of education and the opinion that they hold with regard to their abilities.

Respondents had different opinions about continuing their work till retirement. A majority of them wanted to continue their work even after their retirement. Another aspect, which was evident from their response was that education did not significantly influence their opinion in this regard.

Table 2. Association between Education of the Respondents and Opinion of their Family and Society

Variable	*x^2 Value*	*Significance*
Do family and friends appreciate	0.43881	0.80300
Is husband co-operative	1.24377	0.87084
Whether in-laws co-operate	3.66876	0.72140
Reaction of husbands/parents for working with men	8.16569	0.41745
Whether they have gained the confidence of society	4.08643	0.12961

On questioning the respondents about the appreciation they get from the family and society, the responses showed no significant association with their education. Husbands and in-laws of a policewoman in general had certain views about the police profession. Working hours, men colleagues etc. are certain aspects of the profession that the family did not accept whole-heartedly. This situation is the same even if the respondent is educated. At the same time, the appreciation they receive from the society is only for their deeds, such as solving problems and helping victims etc. and not for their level of education.

Table 3. Association between Education of the Respondents and the Opinion of Society

Comparison	*Chi-Square Value*	*Significance*
Recognition in society with respect to education	8.06585	0.01

Statistical analysis shows a significant association between the recognition of the women police in the society and the education of the respondents. This is so, because educated policewomen know the laws better and perform their duties abiding by the law. Thus, the society recognizes them more and confides in them.

Table 4. Working Conditions with Respect to Education

Variable	*x^2 Value*	*Significance*
Education	0.0013	0.9993

The education of the respondents shows no association to the working condition because irrespective of the level of education, the policewomen have to do similar duties. Questions about working conditions included questions like reaction of the agitators and processionists, etc. Since the duties are similar, the policewomen, regardless of their level of education, have to face the hostility of the agitators and perform their duty. Working conditions also include facilities like weapons etc. safety levels of the job and so on. Every policewoman gets the similar treatment and education does not make the conditions better or worse.

Table 5. ANOVA on Score of Welfare Measures with Reference to Education

Independent Variable	*Mean Rank*	*Statistics*	*Value*	*Significance*
Education	Uptc 10th - 39.91 Upto 12th - 55.34 Graduate - 51.45	Kruskal - Wallis 1- way ANOVA	5.9523	0.05

Statistics show that there is a significant association between the level of satisfaction of the welfare measures and the level of education of the respondents. As the respondents who have completed the 12th standard will mostly be in the posts of Sub-Inspectors or Inspectors after a series of promotions and hence they will have higher levels of satisfaction with respect to the welfare measures. Respondents who have completed the 10th standard will most probably be in the post of constables etc. thus, they are generally not provided enough welfare measures such as quarters etc.

Table 6. Association between Nativity of the Respondents and their Opinion of their Job

Variable	x^2 *Value*	*Significance*
Choosing Police work as career	3.64205	0.30280
Whether Police job is better than other departments	0.16783	0.68205
Whether job suits their ability	0.72971	0.39298
Will continue to work till retirement	1.39430	0.23768

When attempts were made to study the association between the nativity of the respondents and some aspects of their profession, the results proved that there was no association. The aspects that were of interest were the reasons for choosing a career in the police, whether the police work is better than the other jobs, their job suited their abilities and their plan to continue work till retirement.

The general perception of the respondents, whether they were from rural or urban areas, their reasons for choosing this career or that profession being the best, seemed to be similar. They joined the force for ever so many reasons which were not affected by their nativity. The job suiting the ability also showed no association with their nativity because the nativity surely did not seem to have the abilities of any person in particular. They believed that every person has his or her own level of capabilities and their nativity surely has no influence.

Table 7. Association between Nativity of the Respondents and the Opinion of their Family and Society

Variable	*x^2 Value*	*Significance*
Do your family and friends appreciate	0.46331	0.49608
Is husband co-operative?	1.13677	0.56644
Whether in-laws co-operate?	4.16224	0.24447
Reaction of husbands/parents for working with men	4.95728	0.29171
Whether they have gained the confidence of society?	0.00772	0.93000

The appreciation the respondents receive from the family and society was statistically proved to have no association with their nativity. The co-operation they get from their husband or family was the same whether they are from a rural or urban area. The society too, does not seem to confide in policewomen in only one particular area. Irrespective of their nativity, it is the action and the reaction of the respondents that help them gain the confidence of the society.

Table 8. Association between Nativity of the Respondents and their Recognition in Society

Variable	*x^2 Value*	*Significance*
Recognition in society with respect to nativity.	4.82276	0.05

There is also evidence that there is an association between the recognition in the society and the nativity of the respondents. The society in general believes that the policewomen in the urban regions are more educated, broadminded and thus empathize with them on higher levels.

Table 9. ANOVA on Score of Working Conditions with Reference to Nativity

Nativity	Rural - 55.58 Urban - 42.51	Mann - Whitney U-Wilcxon Rank Sum W Test	-2.3325	0.01

Statistics of Nativity show some association with the working conditions. The respondents from the rural regions are more satisfied than those in the urban regions. In the rural regions there are only 2 shifts for the respondents and so if they do not have much work they can leave placing a sentry. In urban regions superior officers check the stations very often thus making it necessary for the policewomen to work in 3 shifts. The respondents in the rural regions also opined that sexual harassment is less in their jurisdiction.

Table 10. ANOVA on Job Satisfaction among Women Police with Reference to Nativity

Independent Variable	*Mean Rank*	*Statistics*	*Value*	*Significance*
Nativity	Rural - 61.23 Urban - 37.73	Kolmogorov Smirnov 2-sample test	2.040	0.01

Respondents from the rural areas are more satisfied than those from the urban areas. The monetary benefits they get are one of the prime reasons. The police job gets them a higher pay than the other professions in the rural regions, which may mostly be agriculture or farming. Since rural people are generally less educated, high monetary benefits added to other benefits along with the powers they possess provide them with high levels of job satisfaction. In the urban areas, on the other hand, the eight-hour shift system, higher levels of work mainly the security, bandobust etc. do not give them much satisfaction. The safety levels are also too low in the urban regions.

Table 11. Association between Rank of the Respondents and their Opinion of their Job

Variable	*x^2 Value*	*Significance*
If Police job is better than other departments	1.50261	0.22027
If job suits their ability	0.87834	0.34866
Will continue work till retirement	0.10702	0.74356

The rank of the respondents had no influence on the perception of the victims because of various factors. Responses to wanting to continue work till retirement were common for a majority of the respondents, irrespective of their rank. It is only after years of experience that the respondents get promoted to different ranks according to hierarchy. So the reasons for joining the police work could surely not be influenced by the rank they are presently in.

From the point of view of the respondents, irrespective of the rank they possess, the family and

Table 12. Association between Rank of the Respondents and the Opinion of their Family and Society

Variable	*x^2 Value*	*Significance*
Do your family and friends appreciate?	1.92343	0.16548
Is husband co-operative?	4.60190	0.10016
Reaction of husbands/parents for working with men	6.82137	0.14563
Whether they have gained the confidence of society?	0.04798	0.82662
Has society recognized you and your work?	1.39898	0.23689

friends either co-operate or do not co-operate. The co-operation and appreciation is not received only by the respondents in higher ranks. The respondents believe they have the same type of domestic problems irrespective of their rank.

Table 13. Association between Rank and the Reaction of In-laws

Variable	*x^2 Value*	*Significance*
Reaction of mother-in-law/father-in-law and other in-laws about their job with respect to working with men.	12.50504	0.01

The reaction of the in-laws towards the respondents working with men varies with the rank of the respondent. When the respondent is of a higher rank, she earns more for the family and her position gives her a certain place in the society, which is appreciated and recognized. Thus the in-laws do not mind their working with men. On the other hand, respondents in the lower ranks face certain objections from their in-laws.

Table 14. ANOVA on Score of Working Conditions with Reference to Rank

Independent Variable	*Mean Rank*	*Statistics*	*Value*	*Signific - ance*
Rank	Constable - 41.85 [Grade-I and Grade-II] Sub Inspector-55.73 and Inspector	Kolmogorov Smirnov 2-sample test	2.481	0.01

Statistics show that the working conditions of the police women have a significant association with their rank. The police women of lower ranks [Grade-I and Grade-II] opined that the working conditions were not very satisfying. This can be due to various reasons. For example, Constables have duties such as security and bandobust, pacifying agitators etc. Hence, they have to work at odd hours, the working hours are not fixed as such, they have to personally face the hostility of the agitators etc. The level of job security is not too high.

On the other hand the policewomen of higher ranks such as Sub-Inspectors and Inspectors opined that they are satisfied with the working conditions. They possess greater powers and so factors such as timings and other facilities become highly flexible.

Table 15. ANOVA on Job Satisfaction among Women Police with Reference to Rank

Independent Variable	*Mean Rank*	*Statistics*	*Value*	*Signific - ance*
Rank	Constable - 37.54 (Grade-I & Grade-II] Sub-Inspector - 50.80 and Inspector	Kolmogorov Smirnov 2-sample test	1.763	0.01

As far as ranks are concerned, the job satisfaction is higher among the Inspectors and Sub-Inspectors when compared to Constables. The flexible timings, their powers and other facilities account for the higher level of job satisfaction in the higher ranks.

Table 16. No. of Working Hours in a day with Respect to Co-operation of Family

Variable	*x^2 Value*	*Significance*
Co-operation from husband	7.74805	0.25715
Co-operation from in-laws	15.88145	0.06940
Reaction of husbands / parents on working with men.	0.4373	0.93

Although the working hours of the police women is a little disconcerting, it seems to have no influence on the co-operation they get from their husband and in-laws. The respondents' answers show that, the co-operation that they get from husbands and in-laws is not any better with lesser working hours, or any better with more working hours. Irrespective of the fact that whether the family co-operates or not the respondents opined that the working hours have no association to it.

Table 17. Working Conditions with Respect to Age

Variable	*x^2 Value*	*Significance*
Age	0.8781	0.6447

The working conditions i.e working patterns, working hours, duties and safety levels etc. do not differ significantly with the age of the respondents. Irrespective of the age, duties are given and hence there is no significant association between the age and the working conditions.

Discussion

The hypothesis that there will be no association between the education of the respondents and their opinion of their job, opinion of the family and society and their working conditions are accepted because the P value is more than 0.05 i.e. there is no significance in the p-value.

However, the hypothesis that there will be no association between the education of the respondents and their recognition in society and the welfare measures are rejected. For the question on the recognition in society, some respondents said they were recognised while, some said they were not. This by itself proves that there is an association between education and recognition in society. From the frequencies it is clear that as education increases the recognition in the society goes higher. Statistics also show a significant association between the level of education and the level of satisfaction about the welfare measures, hence, the hypothesis is rejected.

The hypothesis that there will be no association between nativity of the respondents and their opinion about their job and opinion of the family and society is accepted, as there is no significant association to prove it statistically.

The hypothesis stating there will be no association between nativity and the levels of satisfaction with respect to the working conditions and their job in general, as well as the recognition in society is rejected as statistics show a significant association. The society recognizes the policewomen in urban areas more than in rural areas. As far as satisfaction levels of the job and working conditions are concerned respondents in the rural area are more satisfied than in the urban areas.

No association is seen statistically between the rank of the respondents and their opinion of their job and the opinion of the family and society. Hence, the hypothesis that there will be no association between rank and the opinion of the respondents of their job and the opinion of the family and society is accepted.

The following hypothesis, that is, there will be no association between the rank of the respondent and the reaction of in-laws with respect to working with men and the level of satisfaction of the working conditions and the job is rejected because significant association is seen statistically. The respondents at higher ranks have better co-operation from their in-laws and similarly their working conditions are better. Thus, they are more satisfied than others in the lower ranks.

It is also statistically seen that there is no association between the number of working hours of the respondents and the co-operation of their family.

Similarly, it is also seen that there is no association between the working conditions of the respondents and their age.

Hence, the above two hypotheses are accepted.

Victims/Complainants

(i) There is no association between the time taken to report by victims/complainants and

(a) the education of the victims/complainants
(b) the occupation of the victims/complainants
(c) the income of victims/complainants
(d) the nativity of victims/complainants

(ii) There is no association between the reasons for delay in reporting by the victims/complainants and
(a) the education of the victims/complainants
(b) the occupation of the victims/complainants
(c) the income of victims/complainants
(d) the nativity of victims/complainants

(iii) There is no association between the treatment at the police station and
(a) the age of the victims/complainants
(b) the education of victims/complainants.
(c) the occupation of the victims/complainants
(d) the community of victims/complainants

Table 18. Time Taken to Report the Crime with Respect to Education, Occupation and Income

Variable	*Mean Rank*	*Statistics*	*X^2 Value*	*Significance*
Education	Upto 10th - 51.20 Upto 12th - 61.72 Graduate - 48.47	Kruskal Wallis-1-Way ANOVA	3.3475	0.1875
Occupation	Unemployed - 44.91 Coolie - 60.22 Employed - 50.41 (as officers etc.)	Kruskal Wallis-1-Way ANOVA	4.1180	0.1276
Income	< Rs. 1000 - 51.65 Rs.1000 to - 58.20 Rs. 2000 >= Rs. 2000 - 53.98	Mann-Whitney-U Test	0.9174	0.6321

The education of the respondents does not influence the time taken by the respondent to report the crime. Whether they have completed high school or graduation, the respondents had some similar reasons for either reporting immediately or late. If the respondent was bold and had been through too much torture, it can be expected from her to report the crime immediately. However, most victims fearing the reaction of the society and the repercussions do not immediately report the crime.

On a similar note, neither do the occupation nor the income of the respondents make any difference on the time taken by them to report the crime.

Table 19. ANOVA on Time Taken to Report by Victims/ Complainants with Reference to Nativity

Independent Variable	*Mean Rank*	*Statistics*	*X^2 VALUE*	*Signific-ance*
Nativity	Rural - 46.23 Urban - 62.77	Mann - Whitney U-Wilcxon Rank Sum W Test	-2.8005	0.01

There is a significant association between the nativity of the respondents and the delay in reporting the crime. It may be that, the respondents from the urban areas are more educated, hence they try to fight the crime themselves or hesitate to report due to societal pressure. This could be the reason for the higher number of respondents in urban areas who delay reporting. While, on the other hand, respondents from the rural areas might be weak to fight against their family or husband and so immediately look up to the police for help without any delay.

Table 20. Reasons for Delay in Reporting with Respect to Education, Income, Occupation and Nativity

Variable	*x^2 Value*	*Significance*
Education	2.5020	0.28612
Income	0.3222	0.85119
Occupation	0.6762	0.71311
Nativity	2.6060	0.10646

The education or occupation or income of the victims shows no significant association to the delay in reporting because, victims who come to the All Women Police Stations are generally women victims of domestic violence. The victims usually are apprehensive about complaining against their husband or in-laws, which by and large accounts for the delay in reporting the crime. These apprehensions are not in any way different from the educated victims and the uneducated. The same is the case with occupation and income of the victims.

Table 21. Treatment at Police Station with Respect to Age, Education, Occupation and Community

Variable	*Mean Rank*	*Statistics*	*X^2 Value*	*Significance*
Age	Upto 25 yrs - 63.58 25-50 yrs - 51.76 above 50 yrs - 49.04	Kruskal Wallis - 1-Way ANOVA	3.9006	0.8696
Education	Upto 5th - 58.85 Upto 12th - 49.21 Graduation - 52.38	Kruskal Wallis - 1-Way ANOVA	2.2670	0.5079
Occupation	Unemployed - 52.78 Housemaid - 54.06 Employed - 55.84 (as officers etc.)	Kruskal Wallis - 1-Way ANOVA	0.1323	0.0781
Community	SC/ST - 49.85 MBC - 58.46 BC - 54.89 Others - 63.38	Kruskal Wallis - 1-Way ANOVA	2.0295	0.5968

* SC – Scheduled Caste, ST – Scheduled Tribe, MBC – Most Backward Class, BC – Backward Class.

The treatment of the victims is the same and is independent of the age, education, occupation and community of the victims. All the victims are treated with kindness and the policewomen empathise with them. Their background does not affect the treatment of the victims by the policewomen and every one of them is treated equally. If any different treatment is given to some victims, it is only for those victims who need special care like medical care etc. and even that is not influenced by the above-mentioned factors.

Discussion

The hypothesis which shows no association between the time taken to report by victims/ complainants and the education, occupation, income of the victims/complainants has been accepted because it has been statistically proved that there is no significant association since the P value is greater than 0.05.

With an exception to the above, nativity of the victims/complainants shows a significant association with delay in reporting the crime. The prime reason for this is that the respondents from urban areas being more educated try fighting the crime themselves or their hesitation to report due to societal pressure.

The hypothesis focusing on no association shown between the reasons for delay in reporting by the victims/complainants and the education, income, occupation and the nativity of the victims/complainant has been accepted because it has been statistically proved that there is no significant association as the P value is greater than 0.05.

The hypothesis showing no association between the treatment at the police station and the age, education, occupation, community of the victims/complainants has been accepted because statistically it has been proved that there is no significant association as the P value is greater than 0.05.

Witnesses

(i) There is no association between the treatment at the police station and

(a) the education of the witnesses
(b) the occupation of the witnesses
(c) the religion of the witnesses.
(d) the community of the witnesses
(e) the income of the witnesses
(f) the sex of the witnesses
(g) the nativity of the witnesses

Table 22. Treatment at Police Station with Respect to Education, Occupation, Religion, Community, Sex and Nativity

Variable	*Mean Rank*	*Statistics*	x^2 *Value*	*Signi - ficance*
Education	Upto 10th - 34.62 Upto 12th - 36.59 Graduate - 56.83	Kruskal Wallis-1-Way ANOVA	3.4405	0.1790
Occupation	Unemployed - 32.48 Coolie - 36.17 Employed - 41.27 (as officers etc.)	Kruskal Wallis-1-Way ANOVA	1.7467	0.4176
Religion	Hindu - 35.12 Muslim - 37.86 Christian - 42.33	Kruskal Wallis-1-Way Anova	0.7570	0.6849
Community	SC/ST - 41.27 MBC - 28.86 BC - 36.05 OC - 42.86	Kruskal Wallis-1-Way ANOVA	4.0644	0.2546
Sex	Male - 37.81 Female - 34.34	Mann Whitney U-Test	-0.7224	0.4701
Nativity	Rural - 36.12 Urban - 35.79	Mann Whitney U-Test	-0.0670	0.9466

* SC – Scheduled Caste, ST – Scheduled Tribe, MBC – Most Backward Class, BC – Backward Class.

The witnesses in the police station are generally treated with respect and dignity. The treatment does not change with their educational, occupational backgrounds or their religion, community, sex or nativity. The witnesses are given the respect they deserve irrespective of any factor and the policewomen vouched for this fact.

Table 23. ANOVA on Treatment at the Police Station of the Witnesses with Reference to Income

Independent Variable	*Mean Rank*	*Statistics*	*Value*	*Signific - ance*
Income	<Rs.1000 - 28.56 Rs.1000 to Rs. 2000 - 45.08 >Rs. 2000 - 34.83	Kruskal Wallis 1-Way ANOVA	8.4309	0.01

The treatment the witnesses receive shows a very significant correlation to their monthly income. Individuals with a lower income are not treated very well. Aside, witnesses with higher income are given preferential treatment.

Discussion

No significant association is noticed between the treatment meted out at the police station and the education, occupation, religion, community, sex and the nativity of the witnesses. Hence, the hypothesis is accepted.

However, the hypothesis that there is no association between the treatment at the police station and the income of the witnesses is rejected as a significant association is seen.

Accused

(i) There is no association between the treatment at the time of arrest and

- (a) the age of the accused
- (b) the education of the accused
- (c) the occupation of the accused.
- (d) the religion of the accused.
- (e) the community of the accused
- (f) the income of the accused

(ii) There is no association between the treatment at the police station and

- (a) the age of the accused
- (b) the education of the accused
- (c) the occupation of the accused.
- (d) the religion of the accused.
- (e) the community of the accused
- (f) the income of the accused

Table 24. Treatment at the Time of Arrest with Respect to Age, Education, Occupation, Religion, Community and Income

Variable	*Mean Rank*	*Statistics*	x^2 *Value*	*Significance*
Age	Below 40 yrs - 28.22 Above 40 yrs - 31.92	Kruskal Wallis-1-Way ANOVA	0.5625	0.4533
Education	Upto 5th Std. - 28.24 Upto 12th Std. - 30.73 Graduation - 26.33	Kruskal Wallis-1-Way ANOVA	0.5437	0.7620
Occupation	Unemployed - 29.64 Housemaid - 30.12 Employed - 25.46 (as officers etc.)	Kruskal Wallis-1-Way ANOVA	0.9231	0.6303

(contd.)

Variable	Mean Rank	Statistics	x^2 Value	Significance
Religion	Hindu - 29.19 Muslim - 16.00 Christian - 39.63	Kruskal Wallis - 1-Way ANOVA	4.9129	0.0857
Community	SC/ST - 24.97 MBC - 32.17 BC - 30.19 Others - 21.83	Kruskal Wallis - 1-Way ANOVA	2.6464	0.4494
Income	< Rs.1000 - 31.68 Rs.1000 to Rs. 2000 - 28.22 > Rs.2000 - 25.21	Kruskal Wallis - 1-Way ANOVA	1.7013	0.4271

* SC - Scheduled Caste, ST - Scheduled Tribe, MBC - Most Backward Class, BC - Backward Class.

All the accused are treated on the same levels at the time of arrest. The above factors are not considered for any differential treatment. The accused who try to confront the police or try to escape are treated slight differently but even then the age, education, occupation etc. do not stop the police women from apprehending them.

Table 25. Treatment at Police Station with Respect to Age, Education, Occupation, Religion, Community and Income

Variable	Mean Rank	Statistics	x^2 Value	Significance
Age	Below 40 yrs - 28.22 Above 40 yrs - 29.58	Kruskal Wallis - 1-Way ANOVA	0.0193	0.8896
Education	Upto 5th Std. - 30.09 Upto 12th Std.- 29.57 Graduation - 21.67	Kruskal Wallis - 1-Way ANOVA	1.3568	0.5079
Occupation	Unemployed - 36.79 Housemaid - 30.41 Employed - 20.81 (as officers etc.)	Kruskal Wallis - 1-Way ANOVA	5.0988	0.0781
Religion	Hindu - 28.93 Muslim - 12.50 Christian - 46.38	Kruskal Wallis - 1-Way ANOVA	8.5488	0.0139
Community	SC/ST - 25.77 MBC - 28.61 BC - 32.45 Others - 23.33	Kruskal Wallis - 1-Way ANOVA	1.8840	0.5968
Income	< Rs.1000 - 32.46 Rs.1000 to Rs. 2000 - 29.72 > Rs. 2000 - 21.89	Kruskal Wallis - 1-Way ANOVA	3.7810	0.1510

* SC - Scheduled Caste, ST - Scheduled Tribe, MBC - Most Backward Class, BC - Backward Class.

The accused are not treated differently on the basis of their age, education, occupation, religion, community or nativity at the police station. An accused is an accused, no matter what he is and is given the treatment he deserves. No different treatments like underhanded treatment for some, and special treatment for others is given.

Discussion

There is no significant association between the treatment at the time of arrest and the age, education, occupation, religion, community, income of the accused. Similarly, no association is noticed between the treatment at the police station and the above variables.

Hence both the hypotheses are accepted.

Conclusion

The parents of the Women Police extend their wholehearted support to them since their daughters are working in Government and the agency in which they are working is also having enforcement powers. Once Women Police get married to the male colleagues they receive moral support since their husbands understand the various difficulties of their work culture. Whenever they get married to non-policemen they struggle to get wholehearted support both from their husbands and in-laws. But the services of women police are accepted by the society by and large.

The complaints and victims generally expressed their satisfaction that their complaints were well attended. They were patiently heard, comforted, consolded and counseled by the women police. The witnesses have responded that they were treated with dignity, respect, and politeness in the police stations. The accused had stated that they were not subjected to torture by the women police during interrogation and ill treatment like handcuffing during the arrest was not done by them.

6

Summary and Conclusion

Summary

A summary on the research study conducted on the evaluation of the performance of women police, particularly in the region of Tamil Nadu along with the major findings of the study are presented below.

In this study the importance of women in the police force has been projected. The researcher through his study has also featured the hardships, struggles and hurdles faced by them in over-coming the social stigma of women in earlier times being subjected only to feminine task bringing about a breakthrough in the police service. Even after entry into the police service, their acceptance was not whole hearted in the male dominated organization and the women police were restricted only to sensitive tasks of dealing with juveniles, female offenders and clerical support to male officers. Men were neither prepared to induct women straightaway into the police force nor did they like to share the power with them.

But today in the modern society, after overcoming the conflicts between the traditional and modern rules, the women police have proved themselves, equaling themselves to men police and gaining recognition, in proving their merit in dealing with all important cases related to women.

The need and significance of women police in dealing with the increasing rate of criminality by women and juvenile criminality has also been established in this study. Last but not the least, women police are performing with complete dynamism and spirit, proving their indispensability.

Describing the reforms of women police across various states in India, the changing dimension of police force, with more women engaging themselves in illegal activities like agitation, riots, has been featured. The need to have women police has increased with the increasing number of women accused criminals and victims of crime.

Keeping the above factors in mind, this study also summarises the fact that, in spite of their efficiency, the use of their potentialities, is yet to be fully utilized. Conclusively the need to undertake this study, by evaluation of the performance of women police in the state of Tamil Nadu has been highlighted inclusively. This study has been furthermore processed by invoked details on perception of complainants/victims/witnesses, accused and their attitude towards women police. Furthermore some important objectives that give details about the history of women police, characteristics, their difficulties in family and society, working conditions and facilities provided to them by the department etc. have been considered.

Attitude of the victims/accused/complainants towards women police, the reporting behavior of victims, their treatment by the women police in the police station are some of the objectives in brief which were considered to complete this study on women police.

Further, the methodological aspect of this study which has been categorized under evaluation research has been carried forward by conducting interviews with the prime people involved namely the women police in Tamil Nadu and witnesses, accused and victims who were subjected to treatment by the women police. Further the interview schedule was constructed by taking certain key variables, covering highly descriptive and comprehensive questions with respect to (i) profile of the women police namely their age, sex and educational qualifications (ii) questions pertaining to reasons for choosing police work as career, level of job satisfaction, their problems at work etc.

With respect to the attitude of women police towards victims/complainants, questions regarding duration of their wait at the police stations, time taken by the victims to report the crime to the police, treatment given to the victims/complainants and the comfort and consolation shown towards them were queried.

Miscellaneously, questions on general opinion of victims/ complainants about the performance of women police, discrimination and treatment of the women police by their superiors etc. were supplemented. The universe of the sample was considered to be (a)women police (b) the victims/

complainants (c) witnesses and (d) the accused in the districts of Tamil Nadu mainly from the four districts of Chennai, Villupuram, Kancheepuram and Vellore who have reported cases in the year of 1999 in All Women Police Stations. The simple random sampling method was adopted to choose the sample of victims/complainants, witnesses and the accused from the total list obtained from four district police stations in one year. The constructed interview schedule was then tested by its application to a pilot study, whereby its reliability and validity was tested with 20 women police, 30 victims/complainants, 30 witnesses and 30 accused.

The data collected through this interview schedule was then analysed using appropriate statistical tools to deduce suitable results. The statistical tools suitable for this particular analysis was found to be frequency analysis which helped in understanding the bio-demographic details of the respondents namely their profile, working conditions and welfare measures. Secondly, correlation analysis was carried out to a larger extent, which helped in understanding the two variables considering the relation between the two i.e. whether they influenced each other. Followed by this, Chi-square analysis was applied to determine the degree of association between the variables.

The analysis carried out helped in portraying a contrast of results concerning the women police. While majority of the respondents responded favorably that their job was better in many ways when compared to jobs in other departments, they also did not deny the fact that they had to endure hectic working hours with absolutely no rest. It also helped in gaining knowledge about the level of their job satisfaction which was found to be considerably high with the exception of a few, who felt that they were not given jobs equivalent to that of men. Similarly, a majority of them have also confirmed that they face no discrimination in their workplace from their superiors, whereas the remaining felt that they were subjected to gender inequality when any task was assigned to them. With regard to the benefit and facilities provided to the women police, it was surprising to know that, a majority of them were not satisfied with the facilities provided to them and their problems were never attended to.

As far as the opinion of the victims/witnesses towards women police was concerned, they replied in favour of the women police clearly stating that they were given immediate response for their complaint in the police station and care and sympathy was shown to them while processing the complaint.

But in cases of the accused and witnesses, some replies received were not in favour of the women police. Definite conclusions accumulated and derived after a thorough analysis of this study have been enumerated in the following pages.

Major Findings

The present research has brought out some significant findings with respect to women police, which are enumerated below:

(i) Profile of the women police

(a) Women police as such are satisfied with their jobs but not with their working conditions which entail them to long working hours, insufficient facilities, inadequate welfare measures etc.

(b) Women police are not allowed to work independently without any interference from their superiors and other influential persons, while at their work.

(c) The discrimination on the basis of sex while assigning task to them or job placement for them was meager.

(d) Neither are they given adequate medical facilities nor are they provided medical aid in cases of emergency.

(e) With regard to any help and assistance from their superiors while discharging their duties, the response received is negative.

(ii) Some positive conclusions derived were

(a) Women police are satisfied with the level of safety in their work.

(b) Women police are seldom subjected to sexual harassment at their place of work.

(c) The treatment received by the women police in their department is comparatively better than that received by the male police.

(d) Their parents, husbands and in-laws are not happy with the jobs of the women police, their long working hours and their working with men folk.

These conditions precipitate unhappiness in the family.

(e) Women police are better recognised in society and in turn the society expects better performance from them.

Over and above, it has been concluded that inspite of the disadvantages faced by the' women police, those with a higher level of education enjoyed higher designations in the force with better working conditions.

(iii) Women police with respect to victims

With respect to studying the attitude of victims towards women police, some of the primary findings derived were:

(a) Majority of the victims who came to report their cases in the police stations were between the age group of 25 to 50 years.

(b) With respect to their family pattern, the majority of them belonged to nuclear families with the exception of some that were in joint families.

(c) The victims were satisfied with the immediate response to their complaints by the women police.

(d) The victims' delay in reporting the crime to the police is mainly due to the victims' efforts in settling the issue by themselves.

(e) The women police show care and sympathy to the victims when they lodge their complaints and do not use abusive language.

(f) With the exception of a few reasons like the victims not being given immediate medical aid at hospitals and counselling by the women police to the victims only in cases of family matter, the victims were satisfied with the performance of women police to a large extent.

(iv) Attitude of the witness towards women police

With respect to the treatment of the witness by the women police, the following were the conclusions:

(a) Since a majority of the cases reported to the women police were of a domestic violence nature, the witnesses involved were generally found to be relatives of either the victims or the accused.

(b) As far as the treatment of the witnesses by the women police was concerned, the witnesses were satisfied at the response or reception given to them in the police station.

(c) Women police treated the witnesses with dignity, respect and politeness during the interrogation of cases.

(d) Women police did not receive any money or compliments from the witnesses.

(e) However, despite the above factors, as far as the treatment of the witness was concerned, a slight contrast was observed whereby the majority of the respondents in Kancheepuram and Vellore opined that they were given good treatment by the women police, whereas other respondents felt that education and income of the witnesses influenced the treatment by the women police. "The higher, the better" was the principle adopted in the treatment of the witnesses according to the opinion of a majority of the respondents in Chennai City and Villupuram.

(v) Attitude of the accused towards women police

As far as the treatment of the accused by the women police was concerned the following were observed.

(a) The arrested accused generally related for committing the offences of domestic violence.

(b) In most of the cases, the accused was counselled before they were arrested.

(c) The accused was not informed about the reason for their arrest in most cases.

(d) During custody, the accused was not provided with proper food in the police station.

(e) The treatment of the accused was not very different either. They were not subjected to any verbal abuse or physical torture, but all the same they were not given a fair treatment in meeting their lawyers or to defend themselves.

The interaction with the women police about the welfare measures to improve their performances for effective functioning, the following steps have been expressed by them. Eventhough the European countries have already attended to the most of the suggestions, and Bureucrats and Politicians are yet to attend to the welfare of the Women Police. If attended they will be the morale booster for the Women Police.

Measures suggested for improvement

(i) Work aspect

(a) The strength in Women Police stations should be in full complement and should not be fritter away with unnecessary duties.

(b) 3 shift system should be followed as work norms.

(c) Proper legal training should be given on Hindu marriage laws, shariat laws and other marriage laws available in Indian Penal Code (IPC) at Police Training School and Colleges and also regular intervals once in six months to update their knowledge.

(d) Circulars of GOvernment National Human Rights Commission, Natioal and State Women Commission, Judgements of various courts on women issues should be communicated to the women police.

(e) Women Police should be employed in Special Branch Criminal Investigation Department and Crime Branch Investigation Department also as par with male police.

(ii) Counselling

(a) Refresher training on counselling should be imparted to settle the disputes arising out of minor family hitches.

(b) The Women Counsellors may be appointed to all Women Police Stations.

(c) The State and District Social Welfare Officers should visit women police stations and inform the personnel about the welfare measures available in the District/State so as to make use of them for the rhabilitation of women in the broken marriages.

(d) The mobile women police unit along with counsellors and social welfare department officers may visit the slums and areas of weaker sections and render necessary counselling to settle the disputes then and there.

(e) Anti-suicide Counselling Cell may be started in Women Police Stations so as to give proper counselling before anyone resort to extreme end at the time of depression.

(iii) Welfare Measures

(a) Transport facilities should be given to bring the parties in question to women police station for enquiring and investigation.

(b) Pick and drop transport facilities should be given to women police to bring them from home to work spot whenever they are called for urgent and emergency duties.

(c) A rest room with recreational facilities and small gym should be provided.

(d) Facilities for mini kitchen for the night duty staff should be provided.

(e) Basic health kit and medical facilities should be provided to attend on women police who suffer on morning sickness and periods.

Conclusion

The women police force in the State of Tamil Nadu was established with the main objective of dealing with women and children. The assumption was that women possess unique skills and patience that are required to deal with women and children with compassion, dignity and respect. Therefore, there is a need to evaluate the performance of various tasks assigned to women police, in order to improve the women policing in the State of Tamil Nadu. Under these circumstances, a research was carried out with the aim of studying the performance of the women police in the State of Tamil Nadu, perception of the complainants/victims/ witnesses/ accused towards women police and the problems faced by them while discharging their duties. A scientific methodology was adopted to achieve the above aim. The data collected were subjected to appropriate statistical analysis. The findings of the study have led to certain broader conclusions.

It can be concluded that by and large women police satisfied victims/complainants with immediate response to their complaints; women police showed care and sympathy to the victims when they lodged their complaints and did not use abusive language. The victims/complainants were also satisfied to the fact that they were comforted while filing the complaint, consoled with compassion and counselled for rapprochement. Further, it can also be concluded that women police treated the witnesses with dignity, respect and politeness during the process of investigation. Based on the findings, it can also be said that the treatment meted out to the accused was a little harsh and they were subjected to certain forms of abuses both physical and verbal. This shows that women police were committed to protect the interests of the victims of crime in spite of the fact that the accused was not rendered that fair a treatment.

Therefore, it can well be concluded that the primary objective of establishing the women police force in the State of Tamil Nadu to protect the rights and interests of the women victims has been realized. Hence, women police can further be expanded to protect the wider sections of women and girls from victimization due to crime.

Bibliography

Ahuja, Ram. (2001). Research methods, Jaipur and New Delhi: Rawat Publictions.

Aleem, Shamim. (1989). 'Women in Policing in India', *Police Studies,* 12(3):97-103.

(1991). Women in Indian Police, New Delhi: Sterling Publishers Private Limited.

(1991). Women Police and Social Change, New Delhi: Ashish Publishing House.

Anderson, R., Brown, J., and Campbell, E. (1993). 'Aspects of Sex discrimination in Police forces in England & Wales'. *London: Home Office Police Research Group.*

Austin, Thomas L. Hummer, Don. (1999) 'What do College Students think of Police Women? An attitudinal assessment of future law enforcement personnel'. *Women and Criminal Justice,* 10(4) :1-24.

Balkin, J. (1988) 'Why Police Men Don't like Police Women'. *Journal of Police Science and Administration,* 16(1) : 29-38.

Barbara, Fraser. A. (1985). 'Law Enforcement in the USA'. *A final report submitted to the Winston Churchill Memorial Trust as Churchill Fellow,* p.15.

Bartlett, H.W. and Rosenblum, A. (1977). 'Police Women Effectiveness'. *Denver : Denver Civil Service Commission.*

Belknap, Joanne, Mccall and Douglas. K. (1994). 'Woman battering and Police Referrals'. *Journal of Criminal Justice,* 22(3): 223-236.

Bell, Daniel. J. (1982). 'Policewomen - Myths and Reality'. *Journal of Police Science and Administration,* 10 (1): 112-120.

Bharadwaj, Aruna. (1976). 'Police Modernisation in India'. A study of Women Police in Delhi. *Indian Journal of Social Work,* 37(1): 39-48.

Birzer, Michael.L., Craig and Delores, E.(1996). 'Gender differences in Police Physical ability test performance'. *American Journal of Police,* 15(2): 93-108.

Bloch. P.B. and Deborah Anderson. (1974). 'Police Women on Patrol'. *Washington D.C: Police Foundation.*

Brown, Jennifer M (1998). 'Aspects of discriminatory treatment of women police officers serving in forces in England and Wales'. *British Journal of Criminology,* 38(2):265-282.

Brown, Jennifer, Sargent and Stephen. (1995). 'Police Women and firearms in the British Police Service'. *Police Studies,* 18(2): 1-16.

Chakravarthy S.(1994). Equal opportunities to Women in Police. *Police Research and Development* , October - December, pp. 21-24.

Charles, M.T. and Parsons, K. (1978). 'Female performance in the law enforcement function'. A Review of Past Research, Current Issues, Law and Order, 26(1): 18-55.

Charles, Michael .T. (1982). Women in Policing: The physical aspect. *Journal of Police Science and Administration,* 10(2):194-205.

Charles, Michael.T., Copay, Anne G. (2001). 'Marksmanship skills of female police recruits: Impact of basic firearms training'. *International Journal of Police Science and Management,* 3(4):[303-308].

Chesshyre, R. (1989). 'Softly, softly', *New Statesman and Society,* 2: 20-21.

Crime in India. (2001). National Crime Records Bureau, Ministry of Home Affairs, Government of India, New Delhi.

Cuadrado, Mary. (1996). 'Female Police Officers: Gender Bias & Professionalism'. *American Journal of Police,* 14(2):149-165.

Dantzker, M.L., Kubin and Betsy (1998). 'Job satisfaction: The gender perspective among Police Officers'. *American Journal of Criminal Justice,* 23(1):19-31

Davis, James.A. (1984). 'Perspectives of police women in Texas and Oklahoma'. *Journal of Police Science and Administration,* 12(1):395-403.

Dick, Penny; Jankowicz, Devi. (2001). 'A social constructionist account of police culture and its influence on the representation and progression of female officers'. A repertory grid analysis in a United Kingdom Police Force. Policing: *An International Journal of Police Strategies and Management* 24(2):181-199.

Elliot, M. and Fraser, Z. (1986). 'Some Organisational Stress on Policemen'. *Journal of Police Science and Administration,* 2(2):156-165.

Fagerstrom, Dorothy. (1970). 'Wider horizons for Police women', *Law and Order'*, 18:81-83.

Fernandez, Manuel Martin (1994). 'Mujeres Policia [Police Women] Madrid. Spain: Siglo Veintiuno', p.159, Language Spanish.

Flynn. E. (1982). 'Women as Criminal Justice Professionals: a challenge to change traditions'. In Rafter, N. and Stanko, E. (eds) *Judge, Lawyer, Victim, Thief.* Boston: Northeastern University Press.

Garrison, C.G., Grant, N. and Mcormick, K. (1988). 'Utilization of Police Women', *Police Chief*, 55,9:32-35: 69-73.

Gerber, Gwendolyn L. (2001). Women and Men Police Officers: Status, gender and personality. Westport, CT: Praeger Publishers, p.224

Ghosh S.K. (1981). 'Women in Policing', Light and Life Publications, New Delhi.

Hanmer, J. and Saunders, S. (1991). 'Policing Violence against Women: Implementing policy changes'. *Paper presented to the British Criminology Conference*, York, July.

Hearn, J. (1987). The Gender of Oppression: Men, Masculinity and the Critique of Marxism. Brighton: Wheatsheaf; New York: St Martin's.

Francis Heidensohn (1992). Women in Control? The role of Women in Law Enforcement'. Oxford: Oxford University Press.

Hester, R.D., Wayne, C., William, L. (1988). 'Psychological Job Stress and Police Officers'. *Journal of Police Science and Administration,* 8(2):139-144.

Higgins, Lois . L. (1962). 'Women in Law Enforcement', *Law and Order.*

Holdaway, Simon; Parker, Sharon K (1998). 'Policing Women Police: uniform patrol, promotion and representation in the CID'. *British Journal of Criminology,* 38(1):40-60.

Homant, R.J. and Kennedy, D.B. (1984). 'A Content analysis of Statements about Policewomen's handling of Domestic Violence'. *American Journal of Police,* 3(2):265-285.

Horne Peter. (1980). Women in Law Enforcement. Charles. C., Thomas Publishers, U.S.A.

Igbinovia, P.E. (1987). 'African Women in Contemporary Law Enforcement'. *Ilorin Police Studies,* 10(1):31-35.

Janus, S.S.; Janus, C.; Lord, L.K.; and Power, T. (1988). "Women in Police Work-Annie Oakley or Little Orphan Annie?" *Police Studies* 11(3) : 124-27.

Jeanne M Flavin, Bennett, Richard R. (2001). 'Police Work in the Caribbean: The influence of Gender and Nation'. *Policing: An International Journal of Police Strategies and Management,* 24(1):56-87.

Jefferson, T., Sim, J., and Walklate, S. (1992). 'Europe the left and Criminology in the 1990s: Accountability, Control and the Social Construction of the Consumer' in D.Farrington and South Walklate(eds) *Victims and Offenders: Theory and Policy,* British Society for Criminology.

Johns, C.J. (1979). 'The trouble with Women in Policing - Attitudes aren't changing'. *Criminal Justice Review,* 4:33-40.

Jones,S. (1986). Police Women and Equality Formal Policy V. Informal Practices?. London MacMillan Press Ltd. (Basingstoke).

Joyce., Lucy. N., Janet, Q. and Michael, E.S. (1977). 'Women on Patrol- A pilot study of Police performance in New York City'. New York : *Vera Institute of Justice (Pre-Publication Copy).*

Kennedy, D.B., and Homant, R.J. (1983). 'Attitudes of abused Women toward Male and Female Police Officers'. *Criminal Justice and Behaviour,* 10:391-405.

Kothari,C. R. (1997). Research Methodology. Methods and Techniques, Second Edition, Wishwa Prakashan, New Delhi.

Krishnamurthi, Latha. (1995). 'Women Police in Criminal Justice Administration - Role Conflicts and Tensions: A Socio- Psychological Analysis'. *Police Research and Developments*: October-December, pp.10-17.

(1996). 'Role of women Police in Criminal Justice Administration'. *Police Research and Developments,* October - December, pp.15-18.

Lehtinen, M.W. (1976). 'Sexism in Police Departments'. *Trial,* 12(9):52-55.

Letter from the office of the Inspector-General of Police, Govt. of Arunachal Pradesh, Vide.No.PHO(R) LSQ /60/ 82-PT dated 7 December 1987.

Lewis, J.S. (1973). 'Psychological View of Women in Policing'. *Journal of Police Science and Administration,* 6(2):105-113.

Linden, R. (1983). Women in Policing - A Study of Lower Mainland RCMP (Royal Canadian Mounted Police) Detachments. *Candian Police College Journal,* 7(3):217-229.

Lonsway, Kim and others. (2001). 'Police women and the use of force'. *Law and Order* 49(7):109-114.

Madhavan Jija, H. Singh (2002). 'Women Leaders in Police on International Law Enforcement Issues'. *Paper presented at 'Federal Law Enforcement and the International Community' at Women in Federal Law Enforcement (WIFLE 2002), Third Annual Training Conference at Grand Hyatt Hotel, Washington.*

Mahajan, Amarjit (1982). Indian Policewomen (a sociological study of a new role). New Delhi : Deep & Deep Publications.

Martin, S. (1980). Breaking and Entering: Policewomen on Patrol. Berkeley: University of California Press.

Martin, Susan Ehrlich (1999). 'Police force or Police Service? Gender and emotional labor'. *Annals of the American Academy of Political and Social Science,* 561: 111-126.

Natarajan, Mangai (2001). 'Women Police in a Traditional Society: Test of a Western Model of Integration'. *International Journal of Comparative Sociology* 42(1-2):211-233.

Peter B. Bloch and Deborah Anderson (1974). 'Policewomen on Patrol: Final Report'. Washington, *D.C.: The Urban Institute,* pp.1-67.

Pinto. (1988). 'Police women's perception of their changing role', *A study on the role on women in the Victoria Police Force (Australia),* Department of Criminology, University of Melbourne (Carlton), Student Paper p.82.

Pogrebin, Mark ; Dodge, Mary; Chatman, Harold (2000). Reflections of African- American Women on their careers in urban policing: Their experiences of racial and sexual discrimination. *International Journal of the Sociology of Law* 28(4):311-326.

Price, B. R.; Gavin, S. (1982). Century of Women in Policing. in Barbara Raffel Price and Natalie J. Sokoloff (eds.) *Criminal Justice System and Women.* N.Y.: Clark Boardman Company, Ltd.

Price. B.R. (1974). 'A study of leadership strength of female police executives'. *Journal of Police Science and Administration,* 2:219-226.

Prussel, Deborah; Lonsway, Kimberly,A. (2001). 'A Recruiting Women Police Officers'. *Law and Order,*.49(7):91-96.

Radford Jill. (1987). 'Policing male violence, policing women' in J. Hamner and M. Maynard (eds) *Women, Policing and Social Control,* London: Macmillan, pp.30-45.

Rao, S., Muhammad M., Shukla, K.S. and Sahni, S. (1975). 'Women Police in India'. *Police Research and Development,* Jan-March, pp.10-11.

Report of the Bureau of Police Research and Development (1975). 'Women Police in India', Government of India, Ministry of Home Affairs, New Delhi.

Roy, Kalpana (1999). 'Women and their environment'. Delhi: Rajat Publications.

Saha, B.P. (1989). 'Police Women: Femininity, handicap? Madras'. *The Hindu,* May 16.

Sarantakos, S. (1998). Social Research (2nd edition), London: Macmillan Press.

Saxena, Y.N. (1983). 'Policing by Women'. *The Indian Police Journal,* 29(3):30-32.

Sherman, L.J. (1973). 'A Psychological view of Women in Policing'. *Journal of Police Science and Administration,*1:383-394.

Sherman, Lawrence J. (1975). 'Evaluation of Policewomen on Patrol in a Suburban Police Department'. *Journal of Police Science and Administration,* 3(4):434-438.

Sichel, J.L, Friedman, L.N; Quint, J.C and Smith, M.E. (1978). 'Women on Patrol : a pilot study of police performance in New York City'. Washington DC: Government Printing Office.

Simpson, A.E. (1977). 'The changing role of Women in Policing'. In Readings in *Criminal Justice,* Edited by D.E.J. MacNamara, Guilford, CT: Dushkin Publishing group. pp.71-74.

Singh, H. (1984). 'Women Policing in Jammu & Kashmir'. *Police Training College Journal, Udhampur,* 1(2):July-September.

Slonaker, William M; Wendt. Ann C.; Kemper, Michael, J. (2001). 'Discrimination in the Ranks: An Empirical Study with Recommendations' *Police Quarterly,* 4(3): 289-317.

Smith, Dorothy. (1990). 'Whistling Women: Reason, Rationality and Objectivity'. *The Harry Hawthorne Lecture, Canadian Learned Societies 25th Conference,* University of Victoria.

Soothill, K. (1993). 'Police Women in the News'. *The Police Journal,* January.

Stalans, Loretta J; Finn, Marry A.(2000). 'Gender differences in officers' perceptions and decisions about domestic violence cases'. *Women and Criminal Justice,*11(3):1-24.

Sullivan, H.S. (1953). 'The Interpersonal Theory of Psychiatry'. New York: W.W. Norton.

Sutton, C. (1996). 'Performance measurements for the Police Service'. *Intersection,* 6(9):352-354.

Taylor, A. (1974). 'Women Police Officers and their Husbands: Both wed to the forces', November 2, New York Times.

Tim R; Troyer, Jennifer L. (1999). 'Affirmative action, Political representation, Unions and Female Police Employment'. *Journal of Labour Research,* 20(4):572-587.

Timmins, William M; Hainsworth, Brad E. (1989). 'Attracting and retaining females in law enforcement'. *International Journal of offender Therapy and Comparative Criminology,* 33(3):197-205.

Townsey, R.D. (1982). Female Patrol officers. A review of the Physical Capability Issue in Barbara R.Price and Natalie J. Sokoloff (eds.) Criminal Justice System and Women. New York: Clark Boardman Company, Ltd.

Van Wormer, K. (1981). 'Are Males Suited to Police Patrol Work'. *Police Studies,* 3:41-44.

Walklate, S. (1992). 'Responding to domestic violence: an evaluation of the work of the "dedicated" unit in D. Division.' *Final Report to Merseyside Police,* University of Salford: Department of Sociology.

Warner, Rebecca L: Steel, Brent, Lovrich, Nicholas P. (1989). 'Conditions associated with the advent of representative bureaucracy: the case of women in policing'. *Social Science Quarterly,* 70(3):562-578.

Wexler. J.G and Logan, D.D. (1983). 'Source of Stress among Women Police Officers'. *Journal of Police Science and Administration.* 2(1):46-53.

Wimshurst, Kerry. (1995). 'Anticipating the future; the early experiences and career expectations of women police recruits in post - Fitz Gerald Queensland'. *Australian and New Zealand Journal of Criminology,* 28(3):278-297.

Woolf Virginia. (1967). A Room of Ones Own. Penguin Books.

Worden A.P. (1993). 'The Attitudes of Women and Men in Policing: testing conventional and contemporary wisdom'. *Criminology,* 31(2):203-240.

Wyles Lilian. (1952). Women at Scotland Yard: Reflections on the Struggles and Achievements of Thirty years in the Metropolitan Police. London: Faber and Faber Ltd.

Yang, J.D. (1985). 'Women in Policing: A comparative study of the United States and the Republic of China (Taiwan)'. *Police Studies,* 8(1):125-131.

Index